Special Children, Blessed Fathers, while intended for fathers of children with disabilities, is an uplifting source of encouragement for any reader. The group of fathers and mothers who share their reflections on faith and family life provide a powerful witness to the dignity and value of every human person. Their collective wisdom will aid many fathers and mothers as they raise their families, affirming the need to stay strong in and nurture their faith.

— Daniel Cardinal DiNardo —
Archbishop of Galveston-Houston
Episcopal Moderator, National Catholic Partnership on Disability

Being a good father is always a demanding vocation. Being a good father to a child with special needs is particularly demanding. Randy Hain has drawn on the wisdom of fathers—including himself—of special needs children as well as the wisdom of the saints to provide this very supportive and helpful book for men who want to be the very best fathers that they can be to their children with special needs. It's a beautiful glimpse into the lives and struggles of authentic fathers.

— Most Rev. Michael J. Sheridan —
Bishop of Colorado Springs

In some ways, this was a very difficult book to read, because it hit far too close to home. But for this reason it was just the book I need to read, and to reread, often. Many years after his conversion, Saint Paul was able to proclaim, "Not that I complain of want; for I have learned, in whatever state I am, to be content" (Phil 4:11). I'm still on this journey of learning, as are the fathers and mothers featured in this book. The joy is that we are on this journey together, for in the midst of struggle, even despair, it is so good to know that we are not alone.

— Marcus Grodi —
Founder and President of the Coming Home Network International and
host of The Journey Home television program on EWTN

For a large part of my young adult life, I have taught others about the faith landscape of young people today, highlighting the critical impact that parents—particularly fathers—have on their children and their children's spiritual lives. Fathers are indescribably important in children's lives, and their importance is magnified in the lives of children with special needs. Randy Hain has provided a masterpiece of practical guidance and encouragement for these blessed fathers in his book, *Special Children, Blessed Fathers*. I love how honest this book is! Randy and each of the other contributing writers genuinely open their hearts to the reader, vulnerably sharing their challenges, while also unveiling the sometimes unexpected blessings that come from fathering God's beloved children with special needs. This motivating and transformational book will be an answer to many prayers and have a positive impact on the entire Church.

— Katie Warner —

Author of *Head and Heart: Becoming Spiritual Leaders in Your Family*

(Emmaus Road)

Author Randy Hain knows well the struggles in parenting a special needs child and has compiled heartfelt stories from "blessed fathers" and others as a tremendous inspirational guide of encouragement. Randy equips fathers to lead with love and embrace their God-given vocation.

— Donna-Marie Cooper O'Boyle —

EWTN TV Host, speaker, and award winning author of twenty books

I recommend *Special Children, Blessed Fathers* be the starting point for all fathers' journeys with their special needs children. As the father of an autistic child, I appreciate how this book helped me to reach deeper into my faith in order to put my and my son's challenges into a God-centered perspective. This book offers great examples of how men rely on God's grace to help them embrace all that comes with raising a child with special needs. I have read many helpful books that explain autism and provide developmental strategies. However, as this book provided me the foundation to understand God's greater purpose of entrusting me with his "special" creation, I consider it a must-read for all fathers who also seek the ultimate Peace that can be obtained in their roles as "blessed" fathers.

— Chad Michna —
Father of a child with special needs

Randy Hain has given us a true gem in *Special Children, Blessed Fathers* to be cherished and shared. Through his own candid experiences and the stories of other fathers with special needs children, Randy has given us a work that is truly inspiring and helpful. This book confronts the realities and pressures these dads face and reminds us that all life is sacred—these special children with unique challenge are gifts from God. Well-done!

— Dan Burke —
Executive Director of the National Catholic Register

Special Children, Blessed Fathers is a true gift for fathers, but also for any family raising or in relationship with children with special needs. Randy Hain and his eloquent team of co-authors have crafted a manual that is information-packed, but also inspirational and empowering. Every father who wants to more faithfully and joyfully fulfill his vocation should read this book!

— Lisa M. Hendey —
Founder of CatholicMom.com and author of *The Grace of Yes*

What you hold in your hands is a gift, and though written for fathers, it is a light for all of us to share. Randy Hain and his collaborators have opened their hearts and given a beacon of hope to all who need it, especially those blessed with special needs children. Do yourself a favor and read this book, but be warned: it's likely to stretch your heart and challenge your tears. This book is a heartfelt glimpse at the true strength of fatherhood. I'm grateful to all the men who shared it.

— Sarah Reinhard —
Editor of *Word by Word: Slowing Down with the Hail Mary*

It's not an exaggeration to say that reading these stories is to witness God's work. It is surely through the Holy Spirit that these men not only accepted disabilities in their beloved children, but also came to celebrate them as blessings from God. This book is positively not just for fathers. It is for anyone who tears up at happy endings and Divine transformations that reveal a deeper beauty often missed in the world.

— Patti Maguire Armstrong —
Author, speaker and Catholic mom

I have long admired men, who, like Randy Hain and the contributors to this special book, have risen to personal challenges with great fortitude. In these stories readers see something quite special. We see Jesus. It is the Jesus who condescends to mankind in humility and love and meekness—the Jesus who weeps with the sorrowful, who calls those on the margins closer. He embraces the outcast with love and compassion. Jesus knows that each of these is a gift to the world, even if they don't recognize it in themselves.

Each of these stories show that same giving heart. And in giving they have received so much more. Each has entered into that humanness with the total self-donation Jesus calls all of us to. These "special needs" children are, in truth, a special *opportunity* for us to all enter in. These men have all seen Jesus in these special children. And they are better, holier fathers for having embraced their gift.

— Dan Spencer —
Executive Director of the National Fellowship of Catholic Men

Speaking as a mom of thirteen children, six of whom are adopted and are special needs kids, I welcome Randy Hain's book *Special Children, Blessed Fathers*. I cannot emphasize strongly enough the importance of a father's role in the life of a child. The father in today's feminist world is often overlooked or intentionally denigrated. In no area is this more evident than with untimely pregnancies, where over 1.3 million babies die by legal abortion each year. Sadder still, search-and-destroy abortion methods are strongly encouraged for any pre-born babies suspected of "imperfections." Randy Hain's book offers hands-on encouragement, insight, and support to *all* fathers—especially those with special needs children.

— Mary Ann Kuharski —
Director of Prolife Across America

Special Children, Blessed Fathers is a must-read for all fathers in the present culture in which the pull of selfishness has seriously harmed the great Catholic paternal legacy of generosity and sacrificial self-giving. This book offers the hope for resurrection of fatherhood and, subsequently, for marriages and families.

— Rick Fitzgibbons, MD —
Director of the Institute for Marital Healing

As a mother of a forty-six-year-old-son with multiple disabilities, I believe *Special Children, Blessed Fathers* will be a tremendous blessing to all those who read it.

— Dr. Nancy Thompson —
Director of programs and diocesan relations for the Washington, D.C.-based National Catholic Partnership on Disability (NCPD)

While this precious gem of a book is written primarily for fathers of special needs children, it would make a great book for any parent—or any one for that matter—concerned about what Pope Francis calls our "throw away culture." *Special Children, Blessed Fathers* will lift you up and remind you once again that every life matters and is entrusted with a special mission to make a difference in sometimes surprising ways.

— Teresa Tomeo —
Motivational Speaker, Best Selling Author, Syndicated Catholic Talk Show Host of Catholic Connection & The Catholic View for Women

Special Children, Blessed Fathers

Encouragement for fathers of children with special needs

Special Children, Blessed Fathers

Encouragement for fathers of children with special needs

by **RANDY HAIN**

Foreword by
Archbishop Charles J. Chaput, O.F.M. Cap.

With contributions from
Joseph Pearce, Greg Willits, Kevin Lowry
Doug Keck, Matthew Warner, J.D. Flynn
Chad Judice, David Rizzo, Bill Jones
and many others

EMMAUS
ROAD
PUBLISHING
Steubenville, Ohio
www.emmausroad.org

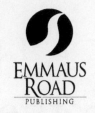

EMMAUS ROAD
PUBLISHING

Emmaus Road Publishing
601 Granard Parkway
Steubenville, Ohio 43952

Library of Congress Control Number: 2015939561

ISBN: 978-1-941447-11-6

Cover illustration by Natalie Rees

Cover design and layout by Julie Davis, General Glyphics, Inc., Dallas, Texas

Dedication

*For Alex, David, Matt, Pia, Max, Kate, Sam, Ben,
Mary Claire, Warner, John, Danielle, Hannah,
Eli, Leo, all children with special needs, and . . .
the blessed fathers who love you.*

TABLE OF CONTENTS

FOREWORD

I have many memories of my own father. Above all, I remember and cherish his love for my mother and siblings. I always believed in it, because it was always there. My father taught me that fidelity was not just possible, but a source of joy and freedom, satisfaction, and friendship. I might have learned that without him, but not in the same way, and not with the same intimacy.

He taught me how to *choose* to love. Fathers choose to love and choose to remain with their children in a way most mothers do not, because mother-love is simply more intense, more natural, more organic. Nothing in fatherhood is as automatic, or as biologically directed, as motherhood. Real father-love is entirely a free-will act of self-sacrifice. Lived well, it gives us a window into God's own fatherhood.

Of course, it's misleading to draw too many parallels between the fatherhood of God and human fathers. God is wholly other, and neither male nor female. But Scripture says, "I bow my knees before the Father, from whom every family in heaven and on earth is named" (Ephesians 3:14–15). And Jesus Himself told us to call God "Father." It's the language God chooses to reveal Himself, and it's through a human father that a child best learns to integrate justice and mercy; to respect and cooperate with others; to protect the weak; to engage with the world; to know our purpose beyond the family; to share the nobility of manly strength when it's ruled by love; and to culti-vate the creative fruitfulness of work. A father's love completes the family, and in that communion of persons the child gets the first inkling of who God is: a Trinity of persons in a com-munity of love . . . like the family.

Looking out from within the love of a family, we can see the poverty of so much of today's culture. If men are simply pred-ators looking to spread their seed and if women really need men only as a way of having children, then marriage is just a contract of mutual utility, with the sexes using each other as a means to an end. But people are better than that. Our motives and yearnings are higher than that.

We live in a curious time. Catholic apologist and author G.K. Chesterton put it best when he said, "The modern world is filled with old Christian virtues gone mad. The virtues have gone mad because they have been isolated from each other and are wandering alone. Thus some scientists care for truth, and their truth is pitiless. Thus some humanitarians care only for pity, and their pity (I am sorry to say) is often untruthful."

Thus we speak admirably of care for the environment and widespread access to health care, of social policies that serve the poor and the disabled, while at the same fostering a culture of selfishness that undermines marriages and families, flees from human imperfection and suffering, and results in the destruction of nearly 90 percent of children with Down syn-drome and other similar disabilities in the womb.

Part of being a good father is remaining sane and faithful in the midst of this confusion. He is the wall against which the inhumanity of the world breaks, the arms which protect the young and weak. Nothing is more honorable or more manly than a father's love—day in and day out—for a child who is "imperfect" in the eyes of the world, but infinitely beautiful and precious in the eyes of God.

Randy Hain has brought together the stories and experiences of ordinary men who have learned to love in extraordinary ways. In doing so, these men offer a witness of fathers of children with special needs that is both memorable and transforming, a portrait of Christian fatherly love that offers a lesson of encouragement to us all.

— Charles J. Chaput, O.F.M. Cap. —
Archbishop of Philadelphia

ACKNOWLEDGEMENTS

From the beginning, this book has been a collaborative effort among caring people who want to inspire and encourage dads with special needs children to recognize what a blessing these children truly are and engage more fully in being the fathers they are called to be. Thank you, Emmaus Road Publishing, for your unwavering support of this project.

When I started *Special Children, Blessed Fathers*, I knew from the beginning that I wanted to invite other Catholic fathers to tell their stories. The book contains contributions from Joseph Pearce, Kevin Lowry, Greg Willits, J.D. Flynn, Matthew Warner, Bill Jones, David Rizzo, Chad Judice, and Doug Keck. Their transparent and selfless sharing of what it is like to be the father of children with special needs is inspiring and a great example for fathers everywhere. The book would not be possible without their contributions, and I will be forever grateful.

Jeanne Lyons is an angel and tireless champion for countless families who have children with special needs at St. Peter Chanel parish in Roswell, GA and beyond. Her work to integrate these children and their families into the Catholic Church is a wonderful ministry and she has considerable insight into the role of fathers that she shares in chapter seventeen. Jeanne is a light to so many and words cannot accurately describe how grateful families like mine are for her important work.

I appreciate the candid and helpful insights from Monsignor Peter Rau, Monsignor John J. Enzler, and Deacon Mike Bickerstaff, who, through their many years of ministry, have seen countless families with these wonderful children and observed the important role of fathers. Through Church teaching and their own experiences, these men provide a marvelous perspective for dads everywhere who are struggling and seeking help.

Kristen Greig is the sister of a delightful young lady named Mary Claire who has Down syndrome. Kristen shares what life was like growing up in her home and talks about the strong role her father Dale played in keeping the family on track. Mary Claire's mother Patti offers insight into the role her husband Dale played from the initial diagnosis to the present, and the powerful influence our Catholic faith has had in helping him live out his vocation as a strong husband and father. I am grateful to them both for sharing a piece of their lives to help other men and their families learn from what they have experienced.

Lauren Warner ("Other Voices" at the end of chapter eleven), Joan McCarty, and Beth Foy ("Other Voices" at the end of chapter thirteen) each provide helpful insight into their family lives and how their husbands respond to their vocation as husbands and fathers. Their perspectives give this book a special touch and will help fathers who read it to better understand the vital roles and viewpoints of their wives. I greatly appreciate their candor.

Maggie Rousseau, the director of the Disability Ministry for the Archdiocese of Atlanta, offers a very helpful and touching

SPECIAL CHILDREN, BLESSED FATHERS

perspective at the end of chapter seven in "Other Voices." I sincerely welcome and appreciate her contribution.

Jan Benton is the executive director of the National Catholic Partnership on Disability (www.NCPD.org), the organization for which all author book royalties from the sale of this book will go to support. This amazing woman has dedicated her life to championing children with special needs and their families, and her contributing story of examples of great fathers is a true inspiration. I am grateful to Jan for the difference she makes every day in the lives of families like mine and for contributing to this book.

Archbishop Charles J. Chaput, Archbishop of Philadelphia, is a man I have long admired for his fearless defense of Church teaching and his devotion to sharing the Gospel. I have also appreciated and respected his stance on behalf of children with special needs and the love and pastoral care he has shown them and their families. As I was considering who to ask to write the foreword for *Special Children, Blessed Fathers,* he was the first and logical choice. I am very grateful for his interest in this project and for his humbling foreword.

Finally, I offer my love and gratitude to my wife Sandra for being an incredible wife and mother. She is the bedrock of our family, and even though our walk is not exactly what we envisioned all those years ago, it is still a special and beautiful journey which I would make all over again with her. I am very blessed.

7

INTRODUCTION

Why write this book? Why now?

I am a Catholic husband, father, businessman, and author blessed with a strong marriage and two wonderful children. My seventeen-year-old son Alex was diagnosed in late 1999 with high-functioning autism. I have experienced firsthand the stress and blessings of raising a child with special needs and the impact it can have on marriages, siblings, relationships, finances, and faith.

As I travel around the country for business or to speak in support of my books, I have consistently encountered one particular problem that is the impetus for this book:

> *Many fathers in families with special needs children are disengaged, in denial, and not living up to their responsibilities.*

Although it is difficult to find reliable data, experts agree that the stress and pressure on families with children who have special needs is significant and the divorce rate is likely higher than the national average, and mothers are typically shouldering the majority of the emotional and physical burden in caring for the family.

As I speak to the fathers in these families (and individuals who know them), there clearly are great fathers out there, but far too many are struggling with some or all of the following challenges:

- Many feel angry and frustrated.

- They often feel overwhelmed.

- They are in denial about the diagnosis.

- They feel a profound sense of guilt.

- They feel severely let down when they recognize that their dreams for their child (children) may not be realized.

- Many focus only on the challenges of having a child with special needs and fail to see these children as the blessings they truly are.

- Because of the financial stress involved in raising a child with special needs, they often lose themselves in the role of provider and ignore the emotional and physical toll on their wives and family.

- They often drift apart from their wives as the energy put into the care of the child and financial concerns outpace the love and care that should be invested into the marriage.

- They need help and good examples to follow, but often they do not know where to turn. Pride prevents them from asking for advice or assistance.

- They often experience isolation and feel they have nobody to talk to about what they are facing and feeling. Some fear they will be perceived as weak if they voice their issues.

- They, especially Catholic men, often don't recognize the power of a strong relationship with Christ and the active practice of our Catholic faith as important solutions to their crisis.

- Their prayer lives are often minimal or nonexistent and they may not recognize the healing power and support to be found in a vibrant prayer life.

This is not a definitive list. Other aspects of the problem exist, but these are the ones I consistently hear from other men, their wives, or those close to families with children who have special needs.

In the fall of 2014, I had just completed the manuscript for *Joyful Witness: How to Be an Extraordinary Catholic* (Servant Books), and with the 2014 Father's Day release of *Journey to Heaven: A Road Map of Catholic Men* (Emmaus Road Publishing), I was exhausted and in need of a sabbatical from writing after releasing two books in one year. But, God had other plans.

I prayed in earnest for weeks during Eucharistic Adoration about what God wanted me to do next. As I prayed I could not get the idea for a book of encouragement for the fathers of children with special needs out of my mind. If men are struggling, perhaps the Holy Spirit might work through a book like this to reach them.

I reached out to several Catholic authors who have children with special needs and found them to be very enthusiastic about the idea. I also have great respect for the example they set for all of us in how they live up to their responsibilities as husbands and fathers. After pitching the idea to Emmaus Road Publishing and receiving their enthusiastic approval, the book project became a reality. So much for my sabbatical plans!

As you read the book, you will find all of the even-numbered chapters to be admirable and heartfelt contributions from Catholic fathers, including Kevin Lowry, Doug Keck, J. D. Flynn, Greg Willits, Matthew Warner, Bill Jones, David Rizzo, Chad Judice, and Joseph Pearce. These men have offered an unfiltered look into their lives as the fathers of children with special needs. The stories are moving and the lessons are invaluable.

In the odd-numbered chapters, I share experiences from my own life as Alex's father, and highlight at times what I've learned from the example of St. Joseph, patron saint of fathers. I also include candid observations from others who share a unique perspective on the lives of fathers of children with special needs. The rawness of these interviews expresses genuine and honest voices from real parents in real family situations. I've asked the editor to retain their voices and avoid editorial polish. I hope you find them to be both helpful and refreshing. Chapter seventeen offers a candid interview about the role of fathers in these families with Jeanne Lyons, an expert on integrating children with special needs and their families into the Catholic Church.

Appendix One There is also a chapter in the book that crystallizes the best lessons and practical wisdom offered by the Scriptures, the saints, the dads in this book, and others to help fathers who are seeking encouragement and help. Finally, Appendix Two offers additional resources that provide the help and encouragement you might need to become the father you are called to be.

The result is a somewhat eclectic mix of candid stories, helpful observations, and numerous examples of how Catholic fathers can and should engage their family's dynamic. This book is *not* intended to solve every issue faced by families with children who have special needs. The intent is merely to show good examples for fathers to follow, provide candid insights, remind us of the power of strong faith, and encourage us to embrace our vocations as husbands and fathers and be the strong men we are called to be. I will pray for all of you and I humbly ask that you pray for me. Our families need us and we cannot fail.

Your brother in Christ,
— Randy Hain —

All royalties earned from the sale of Special Children, Blessed Fathers will be donated to the National Catholic Partnership on Disability (www.ncpd.org) to support the magnificent work they do in guiding initiatives aimed at promoting greater participation of persons with disabilities in the Catholic Church.

1

ST. JOSEPH
POINTS THE WAY

Saint Joseph was a just man, a tireless worker,
the upright guardian of those entrusted
to his care. May he always guard, protect
and enlighten families.
— Pope St. John Paul II, *Familiaris Consortio* —

I often struggle to give my oldest son, who has high-functioning autism, the time, focus, and patience he needs from me each day. I frequently feel inadequate when I advise and guide my youngest son through the minefields of today's culture. My loving wife should expect my active engagement and full attention, yet I often feel distracted or too worn out to give her the 100 percent she deserves.

After a Mass not long ago, I lingered a few minutes to ask for the intercession and help of St. Joseph. As a Catholic dad and husband, who better for me to emulate than the patron saint of fathers?

I have long been drawn to St. Joseph and find in his life the encouragement to be more obedient and trusting in God's promises. Even though I often wrestle with self-created challenges on the parenting and marriage fronts and manage to get in my own way with great frequency, my shortcomings are somewhat lessened when I pray for St. Joseph's intercession and reflect on the heroic example he set in caring for Jesus and Mary.

Reflecting on the life of this great saint often helps me get back on track with my family responsibilities and regain the peace that frequently leaves me when I allow work and the pressures of the world to dominate my thoughts and calendar. I am convinced that focusing on the simple yet profound lessons of St. Joseph's life have helped me be a little more heroic in being a better father to both of my sons, but in particular to my son with special needs. Even when we have difficult days, I find peace and comfort in St. Joseph's intercession.

Powerful Lessons from St. Joseph

- St. Joseph was *obedient* and *accepting* of God's will through-out his life. In Matthew's Gospel, we see Joseph listen to the angel of the Lord explain the virgin birth in a dream and then obey God's instruction to "take Mary your wife" (1:20–24). He was obedient when he led his family to Egypt to escape Herod's infanticide in Bethlehem (2:13–15). He obeyed the angel's later commands to return to Israel (2:19–20) and settle in Nazareth with Mary and Jesus (2:22–23). How often does our pride and willfulness get in the way of our obedience to God?

- St. Joseph made *selfless sacrifices* and was devoted to his family. In the limited knowledge we have about this great saint, we see a man who only thought of serving Mary and Jesus, never himself. What many may see as sacrifices on his part were actually acts of selfless love. His devotion to his family is a model for fathers today who may be allowing disordered attachments to the things of this world distort their focus and hinder their vocations.

- St. Joseph led by *example*. None of his words are written in Scripture, but we can clearly see by his actions that he was a just, loving, and faithful man. We often think that we influence others primarily by what we say, when, in fact, we often influence others by what we do. Our actions are being watched. Every recorded decision and action made by this great saint is the standard for men to follow today.

- St. Joseph showed great *fortitude*. The normal responsibilities of fatherhood can be daunting, but being the father of a child with special needs can stretch our patience to the breaking point at times. Fortitude is a special virtue that "teaches us to appreciate the human and divine value of patience," St. Josemaría Escrivá teaches. "The person with fortitude is one who perseveres in doing what his conscience tells him he ought to. He does not measure the value of a task exclusively by the benefit he derives from it, but by the service he renders to others" (*Friends of God*, 77–78).

- St. Joseph was a *leader*, but not in the way we may view leadership today. After being turned away from the Bethlehem inn, he led as a loving husband when he improvised to find a stable for Mary to give birth to Jesus. He led as a man of faith when he obeyed God in all things and took his wife, the pregnant Mary, and later brought the Holy Family safely to Egypt. He led as the family provider by working long hours in his workshop to make sure they had enough to eat and a roof over their heads. He led as a teacher by teaching Jesus his trade and how to live and work as a man.

Deacon Mike Bickerstaff

Seeking an additional voice on the model of St. Joseph and the man's role as leader and provider, I turned to Deacon Mike Bickerstaff, who is assigned to St. Peter Chanel Catholic Church in the Archdiocese of Atlanta and serves as St. Peter's director of Adult Education and Evangelization. He is also the co-founder and editor-in-chief of the Integrated Catholic Life eMagazine (www. IntegratedCatholiclife.org), as well as a happily married father and grandfather who has observed and worked with families with special needs children in his ministry as a deacon.

Children are among the great blessings of this life. The family was instituted by God for two principal goods: the good of the spouses and the procreation of children. These children, like their parents, are human beings who possess equal, God-given dignity, made for a supernatural end. It is within the family that these children are raised and educated by their mothers and fathers. It is within the family that they should first come to know the risen Christ and encounter God's love for them, and in turn, they honor their parents.

The Catechism states, "The fourth commandment opens the second table of the Decalogue. It shows us the order of charity. God has willed that, after him, we should honor our parents to whom we owe life and who have handed on to us the knowledge of God. We are obliged to honor and respect all those whom God, for our good, has vested with his authority" (2197).

The Catechism goes on to say that this commandment presupposes the duties of fathers and mothers toward their children. Of course, spouses have duties and responsibilities to one another in the complementary roles of their vocation as husband and wife.

Traditionally, fathers have carried a particular responsibility as a leader and provider for their children. The challenge for fathers today is to identify the duties entrusted to them by God and to give these duties priority over the expectations of culture and society. Principally, a father is called to provide his children with food, clothing, and shelter, and to protect and keep them from harm. He is to work with his wife to educate and form his children to become productive members of the community, and, most of all, he is to educate them about the God who loves them and introduce them to His ways.

Among the many virtues of St. Joseph, his qualities and example as leader and provider can be a powerful and effective model for today's fathers.

Leaders get their priorities right. It is fundamental. The metrics by which today's culture measures the success of a father differs from God's expectation. If we are going to pass on to our children the higher virtues—humility, integrity, compassion, kindness, dependability, honor, faithfulness—we need to practice them . . . every hour of every day, even when life comes at us in ways we do not expect.

We first get to know St. Joseph in Matthew's Gospel. In the genealogy, Joseph is identified as the husband of Mary. We are told of his reaction when he learned that Mary was with child. Described as a righteous man and wanting to avoid bringing shame to her, he sought to do the right thing. How many times in our lives are we disappointed when people and events do not appear to live up to our expectations? Notice that what appeared to be a betrayal of Joseph by Mary was nothing of the sort.

Compared to the norms of his day, his desire to respond with compassion was evidence of the foundation of virtue that allowed his relationship with Mary to continue. His love of Mary and openness to God's grace allowed him to receive the word of the angel and be at peace.

Joseph was told by the angel that he was to name the child Jesus, and that Jesus would be "God with us." Naming the child signifies the authority given to Joseph over the child. Along with this authority (responsibility) came the blessing of the intimate presence of God in his life!

Leaders and providers know what to do and how to react when circumstances dictate a change of course.

Joseph did what was necessary when faced with the difficult journey to Bethlehem. Caring for his pregnant wife, he persisted in the face of rejection upon rejection until a place was secured for Mary to give birth to the Savior. He watched over her as strangers came to pay homage and bestow gifts. As if that difficult journey was not enough, the cruel treachery of Herod unleashed upon the innocents of Bethlehem forced Joseph to flee with his family to Egypt as refugees until it was safe for them to return home. Mary and Jesus were able to depend on Joseph when they most needed him.

When Mary and Joseph discovered that their twelve-year-old son was apparently left behind in Jerusalem, the courage and calm reason of Joseph (and Mary) in the face of great stress allowed them to do what was necessary to find their 'lost' boy.

There are two points (among others) to consider about the life and example of Joseph. First, even though Joseph was the foster father of the Son of God, life was not easy. Joseph was continually challenged, sometimes in desperate circumstances, to provide the same essentials to his family that all fathers are called by God to provide. Second, being true to his calling, Joseph was incredibly blessed by the gift of the Christ child. Imagine for a moment, the son that Joseph taught carpentry is the same person who placed the stars and planets in space. The joy that Joseph knew and shared with Mary must have been indescribable. This same joy and blessing is waiting for all fathers who lead and provide for their families in accord with God's will.

2

JOY IN TRIBULATIONS
Kevin Lowry

We are afflicted in every way, but not crushed;
perplexed, but not driven to despair, persecuted,
but not forsaken; struck down, but not destroyed.
— 2 Corinthians 4:8–9 —

I'll never forget the day we found out something was up with our seventh child.

My wife was about five months pregnant at the time. Her OB-GYN called me at the office. Now, he's a good guy, but he had never called me at the office. Personally. Ever. Our conversation was short. "She's measuring too large for gestational age; it's called Polyhydramnios. It's sometimes associated with Down syndrome. We'll have to do some testing."

To us, Down syndrome didn't seem like the end of the world. We had some close friends with a daughter with Down syndrome who was (and is) an amazing person. We prayed, and proceeded with the testing. It wasn't Down syndrome. In some ways, it was worse.

The baby had heterotaxy, and what they called Polysplenia Syndrome—conditions so rare that our pediatrician hadn't even heard of them. Basically, there were internal structural anomalies, and the baby would require surgery upon birth. If he survived. Beyond that, the survival rate to adolescence hovered around 10 percent, driven by a high likelihood (90 percent) of congenital heart problems.

This is why my wife and I came to mourn for a baby who hadn't even been born. Yet God had other plans. Our son David did survive his birth, along with a surgery performed shortly thereafter. He survived . . . and through the prayers of countless people (most notably the late Fr. Ray Ryland), David dodged the severe congenital heart problems that cause the high mortality rate for Heterotaxy kids.

Of course, that doesn't mean that David has an easy life. His condition requires close monitoring, and serious risks remain. After a few years of relative calm, he has undergone four surgeries in the last several months, and it looks like he needs yet another one. Lord, have mercy.

As a father, one of the things I've pondered over the years is how to handle such challenges as a Christian. Here's a Scripture passage that hit me like a brick in the face, describing how the Apostles dealt with challenges after running afoul of the Sanhedrin:

> After recalling the apostles, they had them flogged, ordered them to stop speaking in the name of Jesus, and dismissed them. So they left the presence of the Sanhedrin, rejoicing that they had been found worthy to suffer dishonor for the sake of the name. And all day long, both at the temple and in their homes, they did not stop teaching and proclaiming the Messiah, Jesus. (Acts 5:40–42, NAB)

The Sanhedrin had them *flogged*! And they left *rejoicing*! Can you imagine? For most of us, the thought of rejoicing over a flogging just doesn't compute. It's also clear from the passage that the apostles weren't dissuaded from their mission. They continued to teach and proclaim. Apparently another flogging—or worse—wasn't a deterrent.

This theme isn't an outlier in Scripture, either. The Letter to the Romans contains another passage that is startling in its assessment of how to handle challenges:

> Not only that, but we even boast of our afflictions, knowing that affliction produces endurance, and endurance, proven character, and proven character, hope, and hope does

not disappoint, because the love of God has
been poured out into our hearts through
the holy Spirit that has been given to us.
(Rom 5:3–5, NAB)

So here we have *afflictions* (via endurance and proven character) causing *hope*. Not exactly intuitive stuff, right? The mind
reels. Some translations of the Bible, rather than "boast of our
afflictions," say, "joy in tribulations." Just how does that work?

Being thankful during difficult times is hard, even with a
healthy family. Have you ever tried it? It's really a reflection of
radical trust, of putting our faith in God's providence. That's
not easy. At the same time, there's even a greater challenge:
what about giving thanks even *for* the difficulties?

This isn't for the faint of heart. It takes enormous faith,
which is truly a gift. But isn't this an extraordinary expres-
sion of putting ourselves, and our families, completely in
God's hands?

Now, a reality check. I'm not saying that we should be happy
when something bad happens. We're all subject to emotional
vicissitudes—that "punch in the gut" feeling we experience,
particularly when innocent children experience tremendous
pain or hardship. Rather, when there are circumstances beyond our control that play out, we can pray that the Lord's will
be done through those circumstances and give thanks for His
Lordship over our lives. Even unto death.

This habit of gratitude to God, no matter what, is really a
major part of spiritual growth. It also helps fathers of special
needs children to grow in holiness ourselves *so we can become
the fathers our children need*. This is among the many ways special needs children can positively affect those around them.

What have been the practical manifestations of having a special needs child in our family? Over the past decade-plus, we've learned a few things. See if you can relate to a couple examples that follow.

It's an invitation to get our priorities in order. I'm speaking to fathers, specifically. Think about your relationship with your wife first. Although there's a temptation to put the significant needs of your child first, that's a mistake. Why? Because your marriage comes first. You share a sacrament with your wife. The children are the fruit of your blessed union. That doesn't mean that they're not important; rather, it means that your wife is super-important.

At the same time, it's an invitation to examine the other aspects of our lives that may be preventing us from honoring our marriage and providing our children with the greatest gift we can give—ourselves. They need our prayers, our time, our encouragement, our direction, our strength. This is tough if we're overcommitted, whether it is in our work, hobbies, social activities, even ministries. Here's a question to ask yourself: if my child was going to be in the hospital for the next two months, how would my priorities change? It's a useful thought exercise to determine how you might rearrange your daily schedule. Pray about it, and don't be afraid to make necessary changes.

I took a new job twice over the years when the balancing act between work and family became untenable. This isn't always the right answer, of course, but in my case I look back on these changes and recognize that God's hand was there guiding us. When I left the CPA firm that I had joined right out of college, I remember that I thought I was taking myself off the fast track. But in the long run, the move was foundational to my career and allowed me to diversify my experience in an extremely constructive way.

Look for the silver linings. Even though this may sound crazy, and the occasion of David's birth was extremely stressful, it had the completely unanticipated effect of drawing the rest of our family closer together. The six older kids all had great affection for David and somehow banded together to help care for him. This had the happy side effect of bringing them out of themselves a bit and recognizing the fragility of life. Perhaps this was true for us all, parents included.

We also decided that the topic of future children was best left up to God rather than geneticists. The odds of having another baby with similar problems was significant, according to one doctor we consulted. Knowing other friends with special needs children who had even higher odds of recurring problems, we decided in our case (after a NFP-enabled hiatus) that we would prayerfully try to conceive another baby. I distinctly remember a deep desire in my wife to have more children at that point, recognizing that the time for further procreation was limited.

We did have another baby and her name is Hannah. She's a joy to the entire family!

One other thought to consider is a lesson we learned shortly after David's birth: when you're in the Neonatal Intensive Care Unit at a large Children's Hospital, you don't need to travel very far to find children (and parents) who are much worse off than you. It's an important thing to recognize, but it's also an invitation to pray for and support others. My wife and I know many parents whose children have died or experienced hardships that go well beyond our own. We're constantly humbled by others whose paths are incredibly difficult, and who often face tougher times without the benefit of faith, family support, or adequate medical insurance.

Special kids make us better fathers. I sure didn't feel that way at first. With an underlying tension in the home, it's easy for us to snap at other family members, act selfishly, or withdraw. I've been there. Yet if we're open to the difficulty, the Holy Spirit can work in our hearts and make us more giving of ourselves, more caring about others, and more willing to lay down our lives (especially in myriad small ways) in daily family life. Medical problems taught me to rely on others, like David's medical team, and to be grateful. His life has taught me to take a less-crazy job and to be humble (I'm still working on that). He has taught me that there's joy in the simple sharing of life, whether we're watching a TV show together, playing a game of cards, or talking about our mutual interest in cars.

For all his challenges, David is an intelligent, funny, interesting, and charming young man. For every challenge we've had along the way, we've been blessed many times over.

I'm reminded of an incident when he was in the hospital for one of his surgeries. Somehow David found out that one of his doctors was a car enthusiast. They got into an esoteric discussion about the particulars of the new sports car engine, but disagreed about certain specifications. Finally, the doctor looked up the answer. His comment was simple. "David, you were right." The pre-arranged penance: ten pushups.

I'm convinced that David is right in more ways than his encyclopedic knowledge of fast cars. He's right for my wife and me. He's right for our family. He's right for our extended family. He's right for our community. He's right for God.

By the grace of God, special needs children can provide tribulations that really are turned into joy. I wouldn't trade our experiences—even the difficulties—with David for anything. I still strive to pray with gratitude, and place all my trust in the Lord for David's future. It's a work in progress, for sure, but so completely worth it.

Need one more inspirational Scripture passage that spells out God's will for your life decisively? Try this one: "Rejoice always, pray constantly, give thanks in all circumstances; for this is the will of God in Christ Jesus for you" (1 Thess 5:16–18).

Amen.

Kevin Lowry is a speaker and the author of Faith at Work: Finding Purpose Beyond the Paycheck. *He and his wife are converts to the Church and have eight children. Kevin's blog can be found at www.gratefulconvert.com.*

3

FATHERHOOD, STRESS, AND BLESSINGS

Count it all joy, my brethren, when you meet
various trials, for you know that the testing of your
faith produces steadfastness. And let steadfastness
have its full effect, that you may be perfect and
complete, lacking in nothing.
— James 1:2–4 —

It is difficult to be a parent today, especially if you have a child or children with special needs. The days are emotional roller coaster rides often filled with frustration and only fleeting glimpses of progress. These families often push the pause button on their old lives as the focus becomes all about therapists, adaptive learning, fighting with schools for support, medication regimens, special diets, etc., etc. The expenses are astronomical and sacrifices are made which other families would never understand. Each day is a battle for survival, which requires fully engaged mothers, fathers, and often siblings to pitch in and make it work. This effort can sometimes be physically exhausting. The emotional toll on the parents and non-special needs children in this kind of family can be dramatic, and is often overlooked in the pursuit of mere survival. The social isolation that often occurs almost becomes a blessing as the family grows weary of explaining their child to friends and neighbors, and they retreat in an unhealthy way into the safe cocoon of their homes where the uncomfortable looks and questions can't reach them.

But, these children are also a great blessing and a gift from God if the choice is made to see them in this light. Once the family finally learns to measure progress in different ways, they can celebrate a positive report from school or when a new plateau is conquered with the physical therapist. Sometimes the speech therapist's encouraging comments about new words being pronounced correctly or an improvement in a social exchange feed the parents morsels of hope that maybe, some day, their child will be able to function in a world that often appears frustrating, alien, and even hostile to them. When the family learns to accept this unique gift from God and stops hoping and praying for a more perfect version of what God gave them, hearts are permanently changed and love flows more freely.

How do I know all of this? Why do I seem to have an insider's perspective? I live in a family much like the one I described above.

There are days when my son Alex will ask us a hundred or more questions about our favorite movies or favorite foods, or try to entice us into several rounds of his favorite board games. Our daily focus to help him lead an independent life and take care of himself doesn't always go as we hope, and we sometimes fear for the worst as we anticipate him reaching adulthood soon. All of this is compounded by the fact that he has an extremely difficult time making friends.

How do we cope? My wife and I pray a lot. We pray for acceptance. We pray for patience and peace. We pray for the Lord to help us be stronger parents and to help us with burdens that seem too great at times. We pray for Alex's future welfare and the future welfare of our other teenage son. We support and love each other, and work hard at having a good marriage and honoring our vocation as parents. We remember to be thankful for the great school Alex attends and the wonderful people at our parish who have embraced him, loved him, and helped him find ways to be a part of parish life. We remind ourselves that God is a loving Father who has great plans for our son that we may not yet fully understand.

The First Day of Advent in 2014 was a special day. Alex has always had a strong connection to our Catholic faith and he especially enjoys Advent and Christmas. He understands Jesus is coming into the world and he wants to be ready. He loves gift giving, and he spent his last dime on a present for my wife that he helped me wrap and place under our tree. We listened to Christmas music as we decorated our tree. He stood a little bit apart listening to his own music as usual, which was okay because he just liked the moment and being with the rest of the family. Later that evening after dinner, he burst with excitement as he said a blessing over our Advent wreath and read the Gospel passage for the First Week of Advent.

That night as we finished our prayers and he crawled into his bed, he smiled at me and said, "I love Advent and Christmas, Dad. This is my favorite time of the year."

My son may struggle with autism, but in that moment all I saw was a child who has blessed my life in countless ways and given me much more than I have ever given him. When he smiled at me he looked like an angel sent from heaven . . . an angel sent to remind me that our Lord is coming and I must be ready with a joy-filled heart like that of my son.

Thank you, my dear son, for teaching me another powerful lesson. Thank you, God, for the gift of this child and choosing me to be his father.

Other Voices

MONSIGNOR PETER RAU

Monsignor Peter Rau, pastor of St. Peter Chanel Catholic Church in Roswell, Georgia, has served as a Catholic priest for over twenty-five years and has worked extensively with families who have children with special needs.

Monsignor Peter, there is a lot of data available that identifies the father as critical to families with special needs children. What keeps some

men from accepting their responsibilities as fathers and husbands in these families? What are
the challenges for them?

My first response is that they might be hesitant to get involved
in parish life for a variety of reasons: not feeling accepted or
welcomed, not wanting to draw attention to themselves. They
usually don't have any expectation of support from the parish.
They rarely mix with other people and so they don't become
part of the community.

From my perspective, the stresses are financial, emotional,
and physical. They worry about their child's future. They are
often exhausted both emotionally and physically from their
attempts to cope with regular daily life while caring for their
child. Obviously, if both Mom and Dad aren't in sync and
working as a team, then tension and stress comes into their
relationship.

When I see parents of a child with special needs working
together, when others reach out and welcome the family, I see
God's hand at work.

What does our Catholic faith call all men to do?
What would you offer to inspire these men to
accept their responsibilities and see these children as the blessings they truly are?

The Catholic faith calls us to respect the dignity of all life, to
be life-giving in all our actions. Once these men can see their
child through the eyes of love, everything changes. This has
been the message of our Lord, that our God looks on us with
love, and once we accept His call to love others, we change.

This is especially important for fathers of children with special needs. It is empowering and supportive for them in their role as Dad and in their role as husband.

If you could sit down with a father who has just learned that one of his children has been diagnosed with autism, Down syndrome, or one of a host of other challenges, what would you like to share with them at that moment?

I would remind him that he is the father of a child, a person. He is not the father of an issue. That being said, it makes it easier to counsel and help the dad to accept his child as a child of God. At this moment it might be difficult for him to see that this child will be a blessing. It may be realized in five, ten, or fifteen years down the road, but it will be a blessing, a gift.

In Ignatian spirituality one always begins with the Thanksgiving Examen, finding the many small and sometimes big things for which we should thank God every day. So for those struggling with difficult news, the effort to see how the person, situation, or event can actually be a blessing is aided by the practice of the Thanksgiving Examen. Eventually, Mom and Dad will come to realize the countless reasons for which they can be thankful.

4

MY GIFT FROM GOD
Doug Keck

*Every good endowment and every perfect gift
is from above, coming down from the Father of
lights with whom there is no variation or shadow
due to change.*
— James 1:17 —

The name Matthew literally means, "Gift from God." I realized Matthew was a gift from the day he took his first breath, but I did not yet know the true breadth of what he was to mean in my life.

I still remember the Friday night my wife Terri and I went to see Matthew's doctor. We needed to know if our doctor had any more thoughts about what was going on with our hyperactive/ADD, semi-nonverbal, four-year-old son. We were actually more focused on how well our talks would go over with the couples we would present to on the Marriage Encounter weekend, our ultimate destination that evening.

I remember sitting together looking at the doctor as he shifted back and forth in his chair, trying to gather the right words. "I hate to tell you, but I think he may be autistic . . ."

Say what? Terri was stunned, but not really surprised; she had suspected as much after seeing autistic author Temple Grandin talk on *Larry King Live* about what it was like to have this diagnosis. Of course, I thought she was reading too much into Matt's condition and that he would just grow out of it. Now I realized it wasn't going to be that simple, but thought there had to be a cure of some kind.

We did not say much as we headed out into the night and drove to the retreat house. Terri was taking in the full measure of what this would mean for Matt and for us as a family. I was still sure it couldn't be as bad as it sounded. But we had a Marriage Encounter weekend to give and that was our focus. In retrospect it was a true gift from God! His timing was perfect! The weekend gave us a chance to prayerfully digest the news and to further bond as a couple who would do anything for our little guy.

I really do not know what I would have done if we had not been led to make our original Marriage Encounter weekend two years before. We not only could hold onto each other while facing this new challenge, but now, more importantly, we had our faith to ground us. Instead of despairing of what was lost, we began preparing for what lay ahead of us.

Terri immersed herself in the world of autism, reading everything she could lay her hands on. I immersed myself in my job. It took me more time to really understand and accept the full ramifications and meaning of a diagnosis of autism.

The biggest breakthrough for me came when I realized that I needed to pray for acceptance, not just a cure. After all, unlike many children with his diagnosis, Matt was at least verbal, if severely delayed. It meant at least that we had an easier road than many who have children who are totally nonverbal and struggle to understand what their child is feeling or going through at any given moment.

We also were given some hope for the future by a doctor at a famous New York hospital. After the doctor saw Matt, she told us she thought he had enough skills going for him that with work he would be able to navigate life better than many of her other patients. That, along with her assurance that his condition would in no way negatively affect the longevity of his life span, gave us hope.

The interesting part about autism, I came to understand, is that these children are not *insensitive* and closed in, but just the opposite. They close in because they are incredibly sensitive to the stimuli around them. One way autism was described to us was that it is like having an FM radio that is constantly switching between stations, never stopping at one station long enough to be able to focus on what is being said or broadcast. This cacophony of sounds is why Matt would fall apart at the mall and in other places where there was a lot of noise or large crowds.

Thanks to Terri, we became aware of a unique therapy called auditory training. It was developed in France and was relatively new. The idea is that you can actually retune the ear drum so that it would became less sensitive to certain frequencies and allow Matt to listen and focus better. It sounded bizarre and I was more skeptical than most—but wow, did it work for him. Matt always was a great traveler in the car because he would just shut down and not pay any attention to his surroundings as we drove along. That is until one day, following his therapy session, when he proclaimed he had never noticed that all the houses on our block had front steps! That was the beginning of a new level of communication that made it much easier for us to understand what was going on inside him, especially in times of stress or duress.

Meanwhile, my daughter Caitlyn, who was less than a year old, began having what looked to be little seizures that caused her to throw her head violently back and forth. Considering her brother's diagnosis, we were greatly concerned that she may also have some difficulties. As providence would have, there was a healing Mass at a local parish and we decided to go. As we arrived, a woman helping at the Mass grabbed Terri and brought Caitlyn and her to the front saying, "Father loves babies."

The priest held Caitlyn aloft for all to see and pronounced that there was nothing wrong with her. From that day on, she has not had another episode. God is good!

Though there was to be no cure for Matt that night, it did reinforce in me a belief in the power of healing in whatever form it manifests itself. For some, healing is physical, for many others it is spiritual, but one way or the other, it is real!

As I said earlier, presenting a talk at the Marriage Encounter weekend literally sheltered Terri and me from the emotional bomb that had just been dropped on us. It helped to shift the focus from us onto how God was working in the lives of the couples there for the weekend. The weekend allowed us to rest in the Lord in an almost contemplative way that gave us time to drink in the actual meaning of Matt's diagnosis. I came to realize this was a lifelong condition that would always be a part of our family's future. As we exchanged our love letters throughout the weekend and dialogued with each other, we prayed to God to give us the grace to strengthen us as a couple. We had to take our "team couple" approach from the weekend with us into our daily lives if we were to successfully deal with creating a new set of dreams for Matt and our little family.

I had realized then that he was never going to play center field for the Bronx Bombers after all. This was especially disappointing; he had looked so good in that little uniform we put him in for the Junior Yankees contest sponsored by a regional sports network I worked for.

The sports business is all consuming, much like broadcast news, and can play havoc on a marriage and family. Luckily, I had recently been promoted and moved to work on our national networks where my life was a little more predictable. Combined with our life-changing Marriage Encounter weekend, Cursillo, and EWTN TV, my focus on life was totally reoriented so that when we did have to confront the facts of Matt's situation, we had our faith to support us. I don't know how one would do it otherwise. You certainly hold onto each other in the beginning, but in the long run you need more; you need a rock that you can anchor your lives to that keeps you from being pulled under.

It was my faith and my godly wife that gave me the strength to live up to my responsibilities as a Catholic husband and father of a special needs child. It was here that EWTN played such a big role as I would tape the TV programs, transfer them to audio tape, and listen to them on my Walkman while I worked around the house. I was starving for truth and couldn't get enough supernatural nourishment. I was what they used to call a Catholic Tapeworm. By listening to great teachers like the Fr. Benedict Groeschel, Fr. George Rutler and, of course, Mother Angelica, I got the sustenance to understand that life was a journey and not a destination, and that suffering had a purpose. God is not punishing us but refining us.

I remember hearing that when something unfortunate happens, we shouldn't spend our time asking why, but what; not why did this happen, but what am I supposed to do now that it has happened. Or even simpler, don't ask why me, but rather, why not me. Am I any more special than all the other people who have their own litany of troubles? A TV comedian once said his mother had told him, "The only truly happy people I see are those I don't know very well!" In other words, everyone has their own trouble, or as we Catholics might put it, their own cross.

That doesn't make it easy, but it does make it easier to deal with. As a father, it makes me take joy in the little things my child does, because for him it is a big thing. I've come to see what is really important in life and what lasts.

I remember how proud I was when I had spent a season as Mickey Mantle's liaison at the sports network where he was doing color commentary on the Yankees games we were producing. I had a book autographed by Mickey for my boy Matt and was so excited that I would be able to give it to him when he grew older. It was the kind of thing I would have loved to have had my father do for me. Of course you can guess that when I finally showed it to Matt he was totally unimpressed. Later he told me, "I'm not really a sports fan, Dad."

I realize this may sound like a nothing story to you but, believe it or not, it helped change my view of the world. I began to see that the sports stars and movie stars I once thought were so important were temporal at best. What lasts is our love for each other in all our foibles and frailties.

Of course, all did not happen overnight; it was a slow process of trial and error as we strove to do whatever we could to help Matt live the happiest life he could. I could have said most productive, but that would be untrue, at least of me. Maybe I was being selfish, but his enjoyment of his life in whatever state he was in always mattered more to me than how many subjects he mastered. That being said, he did graduate from high school and is a voracious reader with a college level vocabulary. That was more a result of his being "bathed in love" by my wife—as one friend described it—than anything else we did to push him.

Still, it was not always easy seeing him fall behind the other children his age or to see Terri struggling to figure out what the best course of action was for him, both medically and socially. I recall the time we took him to the Bronx Zoo with his cousins only to have him fall apart emotionally because the smell of the animals drove him crazy, a fact we only learned later when he became more verbal. At the time, it was a mysterious meltdown with him thrashing wildly about as I carried him out while hearing a bystander offer the advice that what the kid needed was a good spanking! Was it embarrassing? You bet! But in the long run, whether it was his falling apart at the circus, the Raffi kid's concert, or sliding under the table at a local restaurant because they were out of mozzarella sticks, I was the one being pruned. In the world in which we lived, my priority was not worrying about what the world thought, but what the Lord thought of how I was caring for my wife and little boy. It is really freeing when you can stop worrying about what other people think, especially in a society where living as a committed Catholic makes you the odd man out anyway.

An article I had read that really helped me accept things after Matt's diagnosis described taking a trip that does not go as planned. You prepare for a visit to Italy, but when you get off the jet you are actually in Holland. Now Holland is a nice place too, but it's just not what you planned on. It forces you to change your expectations for your trip.

It is similar when receiving a special need's diagnosis. Your life trip continues, but not in the way you had anticipated. Yes there are losses, but the pluses are many and I believe more numerous in the things that really matter. Of course everyone's situation is different and in many cases the challenges they face are greater than ours, but that is honestly how I feel. For a pessimistic New Yorker-media-person like myself, being able to look at our family's world now as half-full rather than half-empty is an accomplishment in itself.

A priest once told me that the secret to true humility was found in being grateful for all the gifts that God has bestowed on you in your life. The trick is to understand which of the many things that come into your life are the true lasting gifts and which are pretty packages with nothing of merit inside.

It is at this point that prayer for discernment on a daily basis becomes so important. Keep your eye on the prize. Eternal life for you and your loved ones is the goal. Everything else is secondary in the big scheme of things. One day I was coming back from looking at some bigger houses further out on Long Island, and I was thinking we should move closer to our Marriage Encounter friends and take a step up in neighborhoods since my career was going so well. As I walked in the door I heard an inner voice whisper to me, "Save your money, a job is coming that you will want to take that does not pay much." I told Terri and she agreed; she was also feeling that we were being prepared to disengage from our work with Marriage Encounter on Long Island.

So that is what we did while we waited to see what the Lord had in mind.

Enter EWTN and Mother Angelica!

I often have said that if it wasn't for Matt, Terri and I would not have uprooted our family—which now included my beautiful daughter Caitlyn—from our Long Island home to make a leap of faith by moving to Alabama to work for EWTN. This statement may seem odd to some since autistic children thrive on sameness, and changing Matt's whole universe in one fell swoop can strike one as counterintuitive or even selfish on our part. But it was the very letting go over the last several years since his diagnosis that gave us the strength to step out in faith and make the move.

It comes down to a matter of trust, as Mother Angelica would often say. You go forward with one foot in the air and a queasy feeling in your stomach. And so we did . . . getting off the jet neither in Italy nor in Holland, but in Alabama, which seemed just as far and as foreign to us Yankees. My daughter originally thought we were going to Albania rather than Alabama, and so in that way she was actually relieved.

It wasn't an easy decision at all. It meant leaving our support system, something parents with special needs children can really relate to. We had come to rely much on Terri's parents and her siblings to help provide a familiar social environment that Matt was comfortable in and could successfully navigate. They were also our only source of respite care in the early days when we were still struggling to adjust to our isolated new world of autism.

That said, we learned a great spiritual lesson when we visited EWTN with the kids to see if this opportunity was something we could really consider doing as a family. When Mother Angelica looks into your eyes and asks if you want to come to work for her, there really is no turning her down. That's how Terri felt. I received my own sign confirming this mission from Matt himself. As Mother talked animatedly to Terri, who was standing next to me, I heard him say aloud to himself, "She is just so beautiful . . ." It took me a second to realize he was, in fact, referring to Mother Angelica, someone who millions loved, but also who most children would not think of as physically beautiful. Then it struck me that my little angelic character was seeing beyond the physical to Mother's true spiritual core, which I had no doubt was a beautiful vision to behold. One way or the other, there now was no turning back.

Ready or not EWTN, here we come!

We hit several bumps in the road preparing to make the move; the biggest was the health of my mother-in-law as she battled cancer. Terri, the oldest daughter, was very close to her mother, and Terri only gave the final okay to leave after she got the all clear that the cancer was in remission.

That left only Matt who, up until that time, had seemed amazingly open to making the move, though he was concerned that there would be no Friendly's Ice Cream restaurants. Plus his only exposure to Alabama style Chinese food had not been a good one. Still, all systems were go until one night about a month before we were to leave, Matt announced that he could not go to Alabama. He gave no reason. We were both stunned. Terri and I had just returned from a second trip and had already put money down on a house. I suddenly got the inspiration to go downstairs and get "Gabriel's Horn." It had been featured in one of Matt's favorite cartoons, *All Dogs Go to Heaven*, and looked like a little French horn. I grabbed one that looked like it in the basement, handed it to him, and said that Mother Angelica would want him to have it for strength. He looked at it admiringly and said, "Now I can go," and so we did!

I certainly do not want to make it seem that our move to Alabama and getting both kids acclimated to our new environs was easy. It wasn't. My work at the network was very challenging at times and kept me busy, and so it fell on Terri to really blaze the trail for our little family in this new world of ours. We were blessed to find a good school district and very loving professionals who helped smooth the way for us over the years. Because of Matt's learning limitations, we knew he would not be able to go to Catholic school as we would have wanted. They just don't have the budget and staffing to really support special needs children like Matt. Surprisingly, all in all, Matt probably adjusted the best of all of us to living in Alabama, and follows his daily routine that includes working at the Religious Catalogue warehouse during the week.

Going through all of this with Matt, I realize that God has given me plenty of support. I have been uniquely blessed to be married to my soulmate Terri for more than thirty-five years and to have a daughter who is a very special person in her own right. There is no way that Matt would be as successful as he is today without the total support and loving understanding of "his girls." My wife is the kind of person who wears her heart on her sleeve, as they say, while my daughter likes to keep hers "up her sleeve." Though she won't admit it, Caitlyn has been a wonderful sister, friend, playmate, and mentor for her older brother since the moment she came into his world when he was four.

Notwithstanding, raising a special needs child, no matter how rewarding it can be, necessarily carries with it its own set of stresses and challenges. Many of these can impact the siblings who find their own childhood effectively disrupted by the family dynamics resulting from these challenges. There is plenty of documentation on the high percentage of broken marriages and broken families due to caring for a child with special needs. It really requires a team effort that effectively starts on your knees! This is where we guys really need to step up and out in faith as the spiritual heads of our respective households. We demonstrate that in how we spend our time and how we love our wives. In many cases, it's one and the same, because just being there to support the rest of the family has a major beneficial impact.

No one ever died wishing they had spent more time at work or even playing golf! Life is lived in the trenches, true bonds of love are built working physically and spiritually together to help each other get through the tough times. It doesn't take the problems or challenges away, but with the grace of God it makes them more manageable. I have found that keeping God at the center of our marriage is the key to weathering the rough seas of emotion that illness can heighten in any relationship.

It is in these peaks and valleys that anchoring yourself to your sacrament and your spouse is essential.

That is where a true understanding of the wonderful gift that you and your wife gave to each other on the day of your wedding can be quite helpful. The Sacrament of Marriage is unique in that it is directly between the couple and God. The priest acts only as a witness for the Church. You are a couple, but one in the spirit at the same time. You were chosen above all others to raise the children that the Lord has gifted you with! Try to remember in good times and bad, in sickness and in health, God will be there to sustain us, if only we ask Him.

For guys, asking for help from anyone, let alone the Lord, can be very difficult. We are supposed to be the strong ones, the ones who fix all the problems. However, in the case of a special needs child there is no *fix*, no solving the problem. There is just living and loving, laughing and crying. It is in the tough, tear-filled times when I cannot see a clear way ahead that I turn to Christ as my guide to keep me on the straight and narrow.

Sometimes when I get down, I read through a little notebook that Matt uses to write down some of his own "wise sayings" based on life lessons he has gleaned from various cartoons and TV shows he has watched. I close with a few of my favorites:

> Give your grief to God and he will exchange it for peace.

> Pride is a roadblock in God's journey to our hearts.

> Prayer keeps your spirit in shape.

> Being a man isn't being strong and tough; it's being good and kind.

Being strong doesn't mean that you try to handle everything yourself.

A wound can stop bleeding, but that doesn't mean it's not still there.

This is also called the gospel according to Matty Boy.

Doug Keck is EWTN's president & chief operating officer and an award winning TV/Radio executive and host with over thirty-five years of national broadcasting/cable network experience. He had previously served in senior level positions with AMC Networks/ Rainbow-NBC and Cablevision in New York. He has been involved in the development of more than twenty-five television networks, including AMC, Bravo, IFC, and CNBC. He has been married to his high school sweetheart Theresa since 1979, and together they have two wonderful children, Matthew and Caitlyn.

5

ACCEPTANCE

*Trust in the LORD with all your heart,
and do not rely on your own insight. In all your
ways acknowledge him, and he will make
straight your paths.*
— Proverbs 3:5–6 —

Not long ago a priest shared some guidance with my wife and me that has been the cause of a great deal of conversation and reflection in our home. In response to learning that we pray every day for our oldest son's future and the healing of his autism, the priest encouraged us to pray first for acceptance.

Let me explain.

He said there was nothing wrong with asking God to heal our son. But, we first needed to ask for the ability to fully accept the beautiful gift of our child exactly as God created him. By asking for healing first, we were in essence asking God to improve on His creation without first understanding the lessons and blessings His gift has provided our family. We have always viewed our oldest son as a blessing and know we could not possibly love him more than we do now. But we may have mistaken love for acceptance as we continued to pray over the years for God to remake him into our vision of a well-formed and perfect child. We have somewhat selfishly asked God to redo His handiwork when we should be accepting of God's plan for his life and trusting that the Father who loves us wants only what is best for him. In the words of Pope Benedict XVI, "If you follow the will of God, you know that in spite of all the terrible things that happen to you, you will never lose a final refuge. You know that the foundation of the world is love, so that even when no human being can or will help you, you may go on, trusting in the One that loves you."

Acknowledging this has been both humbling and illuminating as I think about how to apply "acceptance" into other areas of my life. This period of reflection has made me realize how often, without thinking, I ask God for His help in improving situations and solving problems. Instead of praying for acceptance and discernment about what lessons God wants to teach me or the blessings hidden in these challenges, I have been seeking to reshape the issues into something more pleasing to me instead of pleasing to Him. Do you ever fall into the "acceptance trap" as well?

- Do we see the good that may come from being unemployed?

- Do we accept the blessings of an unplanned pregnancy?

- Do we see opportunities for spiritual growth in our emotional struggles and financial setbacks?

- Does illness (ours or others) offer opportunities to turn suffering into a blessing?

"I consider that the sufferings of this present time are not worth comparing with the glory that is to be revealed for us" (Rom 8:18). It is often difficult to see the blessings and good in any kind of suffering, yet we know from Church teaching there is redemptive power in suffering if we learn to give it up to God. Practicing acceptance may require a radical recalibration of our mindsets as well as complete trust and faith in God's plan for our lives. We must be faithful, humble, patient, obedient, and prayerful if we are to learn the lessons and blessings God has in store for us in our daily trials. We must also seek to glorify Him and not ourselves through the way we deal with challenges, and always express our gratitude for the good *and* bad that comes our way. St Teresa of Avila wrote, "We always find that those who walked closest to Christ were those who had to bear the greatest trials."

I can look back now and see the tremendous positive influence our oldest son has had on our family. His diagnosis with autism over fifteen years ago and the challenges this presented began the long and often difficult process of lowering the wall around my closed-off heart. In the summer of 2005, we moved into the area in which we now live to be closer to his school and therapists. This move began a chain of events that eventually led to our family joining the Catholic Church later that year. The opening of my heart, which began at his diagnosis, allowed me to experience a profound conversion in September of 2005 when I finally surrendered to Christ and put aside the pride and stubbornness that had dominated my life for so long. Without a doubt, our gifted child and his presence in our lives was a significant catalyst behind our joining the Catholic Church and the strong faith our family has today.

Maybe this was God's plan all along for our son. I am just grateful that I can see it now and accept him, not only as one of my wonderful children whom I love, but also as a child of God who was given to us for His divine purpose.

Heavenly Father, I humbly ask that you grant me the gift of acceptance today. Please help me to understand the lessons and blessings hidden within the challenges my family and I will face, and know that I am grateful to you for our lives and the incredible gift and sacrifice of your son Jesus Christ. Amen.

6
TRANSFORMED HEARTS
J.D. Flynn

*You learn to speak by speaking, to study by
studying, to run by running, to work by working,
and just so, you learn to love by loving.
All those who think to learn in any other way
deceive themselves.*
— St. Francis de Sales —

My children are usually waiting at the door when I get home. They bounce up and down and shout to me. They wave and knock on the storm-door to hurry me along.

Most days, while I walk across the porch, they sign "Dad. Dad. Dad!" They do not talk; they use sign language to communicate the things they want the most. "Eat." "Dog." "Music." "Mom." "Dad." "Hug."

It is the last sign, the sign for hug, which gets at my heart. More often than they want anything else, my children sign for love.

They ask us for hugs when they wake, when they are eating, in middle of a game or a song. They ask for hugs at Mass or at the grocery store. When I travel and we communicate by video messaging, my children sit in front of their screens and ask me for a hug.

It is clear to me that nothing is more important to my children than the experience of our family's love. "For a human being," said Jean Vanier, "love is as vital as food."

My children are small. My son Maximilian Kolbe is three. My daughter Pia Therese is two. They're adopted. And they both have Trisomy-21, the genetic disorder known as Down syndrome.

We didn't set out to adopt children with Down syndrome. After years of infertility and miscarriages, God called my wife Kate and me to adopt—and he chose our children for us.

Max was born in December of 2011 in a small town on Colorado's eastern plains. His birth parents invited us to adopt him two weeks later. We knew nothing about Down syndrome. But we knew that the infant in the NICU needed family, and we needed family too. He became our son.

Less than a year later we got a phone call. A baby girl would be born in four days. She needed a family. Her birth parents wanted a family of Catholics, and a family who knew something about Down syndrome. We met Pia in the hospital on the day she was born. She was beautiful. And she became our daughter.

Our story is like the story of most families. In his own way, God has given us beautiful children. We're unworthy, and he made us the stewards of souls.

My children defy the stereotypes of children with special needs. They are not happy-go-lucky dolts or cuddly teddy bears. They are not angels—they are human beings, born with original sin and baptized with the capacity to love as God loves.

They do like to hug. I've made that clear. But they also like to wrestle. With vigor. Pia, especially, likes to read. And Max is the only person I know who wants to vacuum thrice daily.

They take after us, whether we want them to or not. Max imitates the way we tend to talk with our hands. Pia is stubborn because we are stubborn. They pray when we pray, and when we forget to give thanks, they forget too.

They're clever. My children know how to game their father. They know the requests for hugs melt my heart. They ask for hugs when they're about to be in trouble—when they've been hitting each other, or conspiring to steal cookies, or trying to avoid bedtime.

They have the ordinary range of human emotions. They get frustrated. They make jokes. They have disappointments and successes.

Eventually, when you live with children with special needs, the stereotypes fade to the background and you're left with your children, as they really are. As human beings.

Anyone with special children like ours faces unique challenges. Friends of ours have a daughter with profound autism. She requires very special care. Her reality defines the reality of the family.

This is true for our children as well. Leukemia is a common consequence of Down syndrome, and our daughter has spent nearly a year battling two diagnoses of cancer. Her sickness has defined reality for our family.

Little things are the same way. Our children are nonverbal, long after most children are babbling. They depend on unbending routine. They get frustrated with their inability to communicate with other children. They need help eating, and washing, and playing. These are things that define our family's daily reality.

It would be dishonest to pretend that parenting children with special needs is just the same as parenting typical children.

But I look carefully at the children of my friends. I look at the challenges my friends face. Our challenges are different, but I'm not sure we have it any harder or any easier. The difference is qualitative—things for our family are not better or worse. They're just different.

I'm not sure I've "learned" very much from parenting my wonderful children. I've learned some sign language. And a little bit about genetics. And a lot about hospitals. But it would be a sentimentality to say that my children have taught me a lot of lessons.

My children do hold up a mirror to my interior life—my own fears and prejudices. I don't always like what I learn about myself. My friend Fran Maier says of his special needs son, Danny, that "the problem, I have learned . . . is not with his humanity, but with mine."

What my kids do most often is put to flesh what I know is true about the faith. My children remind me of the Incarnation of Jesus, because in the actual realities of their lives, the reality of life's meaning is witnessed and manifested. They've not "taught" me much—not changed my mind or given me pithy or saccharine lessons.

But my children continue to form my heart.

A few weeks ago, my wife and I were discussing our school plans for Max. By some accounts he ought to enter school next year. We talked about public school and the parish school, about keeping him at home and teaching him ourselves. Each has benefits and drawbacks, and we want to decide wisely.

But as we sat in the living room, I felt, in some way, liberated by my children's limitations. No matter what school we send them to, Pia will not become a doctor. Max will not become a priest. I doubt either of them will make enough money to fully support themselves. I do not think they will go to Harvard. Max will not win the Stanley Cup and Pia will not be elected to office.

None of the worldly measures of success are open to people with profound limitations.

If they are lucky, very few people in their lives will worry about their worldly success. Good people in this world will judge my children by their ability to love.

And God's judgment, which is the only judgment that matters, will measure my children by how much they have loved Him, and how much they have loved like Him. What finally matters, for any parent, is whether children learn to love God and neighbor. The limitations of my children make clear to me that love is the only fair measure of a human being. And I am grateful for that.

The decision we make about school should be a decision about eternal life. About how my children will best learn to love. Education is important. But the best kind of education is one that forms children not just to become good producers— not everyone can become a good producer—but to become good human beings.

Shortly after my daughter was born I was sitting with her one night in the hospital. And I was crying, because I was tired and she was sick and the whole thing was overwhelming. A doctor who didn't know my circumstance came by. He told me not to worry, that children with Down syndrome can achieve things, that some can go to college or live independently. He told me that as though a college education should be the source of great hope for me. I felt bad because when he said it, I started to laugh.

College is not the measure of a life well-lived. Neither is money. Or fame. Or even the Stanley Cup.

God's love is the measure of a good life. My children's limitations remind me—daily—that whatever success the world values pales in comparison to learning to love as God loves.

My children's limitations remind me that the decisions I make about my career should be about eternal life. The decisions I make about my family should be about eternal life. The decisions I make about money should be about eternal life. And eternal life is about the love of God.

Max has an electronic toy that he loves. It is a small box covered in plastic flowers. Pressing each flower plays a different song. He can play with that toy for hours. But he lacks the coordination to turn it on. When he wants to play with it, he brings it to me and I help him to turn it on. I place my hands over his and help him to move the switch. Then we play with it together.

Pia loves to "read." But if a book's pages are too thick, or its binding is tight, she can't open the book. So she often brings me books to open, and I help her open the book, to place her hands in the right place and supply the strength she's lacking. Then she can sit in my lap and turn the pages and point to the pictures.

When they bring me their toys they don't have any shame about their need for help. They come to me in confidence that I can solve their problems, and when I can help them, we have an opportunity to share something and to spend time together. I love their weaknesses, because they give us an opportunity to grow in closeness together.

I do not like my own weaknesses and I go to great lengths to hide them. I am disorganized. I am insecure. I am short-tempered. I have a long memory for grudges. I hate these weaknesses and I try to use any measure of worldly success to demonstrate that they do not affect me. I try to prove, as often as I can, that I am good enough, and smart enough, and pre-pared enough to achieve great things.

Despite my best efforts to hide them, I am keenly aware of my sins. But I hate that I sin. I'm ashamed of sin. And so I tend towards a theological idea—a heresy, actually, called Pe-lagianism. I convince myself that with enough hard work—enough effort and good will—I can overcome my sinfulness and my weakness.

My children do not have the luxury of hiding their weak-nesses. Their disability is manifested in their physical features: in their faces, and their necks, and their hands. Their lack of coordination leaves them unable to turn on a favorite toy. Their lack of strength leaves them unable to open a tricky book.

Christ does not have the luxury of hiding weakness either. St. Paul says that Christ was "crucified in weakness." In fact, Christ became man to be crucified in weakness, and his hands and feet bear the sign of that weakness.

Christ's weakness on the Cross brought about the Resurrection. Through Christ's weakness, all of us can be reconciled to God forever. And that's true for my weakness too. My children remind me what I ought to do with weakness and sin, that I ought to bring it God the Father without any shame, that I ought to confess my sins and ask for God's help. Trust—just as my children trust—that when I bring my weakness to God, He will supply the strength I lack. My children remind me that in my weakness, God will be delighted for the opportunity to grow in closeness with me.

Vanier says, "We live in a world where everyone wants to . . . seem strong, intelligent, powerful, up and coming . . . we have to appropriate, to accept the deep wound which is that of the human condition, the wound of our mortality, the wound of our flesh, the wound of our weakness. Hope stems from the acceptance of reality, as it is."

Weakness is a catalyst for authentic human communion. Weakness can bring us into communion with God. But we won't grow close to God, or to one another, unless we accept our weakness, acknowledge it, and acknowledge that we will need help in order to be strong. My children demonstrate that for me.

In fact, it was through Max that God revealed to me the profundity of His strength in the face of weakness. Max was two weeks old when we met him. He had been in the NICU since he was born. His birth mother spent every day with him. She loved him and cared for him. She is an incredible mother. But she wasn't able to take him home and care for him.

On the day he was to come home with us, she sat in a chair and rocked him. She told him how much she loved him. She told him how much she hoped for him. She cried over him. She revealed her heart to him. When it was time for her to go home, without him, she stood up, and walked him to where we stood. The walk was perhaps fifteen feet, but it was the longest walk I'd ever seen a person take. She carried Max to us—and I saw what the road to Calvary must have been like. She placed Max in Kate's arms. They hugged for a long time. And then, knowing that she needed help with her son, she left Max with us.

It was a moment of incredible strength, borne out of the need for help. I pray, every day, that I will be graced with the kind of love she chose. In the moment where she cried out for help, God gave her a beautiful strength.

All told, Pia has spent nearly a year living in hospitals. For most of that time Kate has lived with her. That is a mother's vocation. To nurture a child into health, and into goodness. God gives mothers a special grace—the grace of the feminine genius—in order to nurture their children in love. My wife is a beautiful witness to the grace of motherhood.

And children need that grace. All children need the love of a mother, who will care for them, nurture them, and help them grow into goodness. Mothers are the tender hearts of every family.

While Kate lived in the hospital, I worked, mostly. I worked because we needed the insurance to pay for the hospital and the money to pay for the rest. I worked because the vocation of fathers is to protect their family—to provide, to defend, to shelter. And fathers are also called to lead. To lead their families in prayer, to make judgments, to sacrifice for the good of the whole.

Fathers and mothers are called to different vocations. But the experience of family life confirms how much both are needed. My children need their father. They long for their father's love. And they need their mother. They long for her, too. Children—any children—remind us of the imprint of family life God has written on our hearts.

Finally, a word about suffering. Children with special needs suffer. They suffer ill health. They suffer with frustration. They may suffer with loneliness. My children have reminded me just how meaningful our suffering can be.

When we're baptized we become a part of the body of Jesus Christ. We share in His life, in the mystery of His suffering and death, and because of His Resurrection we share in the eternal life of the Blessed Trinity—the dynamic love of God which will last forever.

Christianity means that we can love with God's own love. It means that we can become a part of God's own life. And it means that our suffering has meaning, that when we suffer, because Christ suffered, our suffering can be transformative in the lives of other people.

When Pia battled cancer we realized that she was called to a special kind of vocation. Tucked up in the sixth floor of Children's Hospital, our little girl carried a big cross. Leukemia is awful. Chemo is awful. Pia was called to spend time suffering. And because she was baptized in the waters of faith, her suffering has meaning.

When she spent time in the hospital we asked friends and family for prayer intentions, and we received dozens of them.

We wrote them in a book and kept them on Pia's bed. We asked that God would use her suffering for grace and we were amazed by the results. We heard from friends whose hearts were softened towards God, who returned to the practice of the faith, whose marriages were renewed, or whose vocations were transformed.

Pia is not a saint. She did not effect any miracles. All of us can offer our sufferings for the good of other people. All of us can unite our crosses to Christ's. And all of us can expect profound results. My daughter has revealed to me the power of being a Christian—the power of the Cross of Jesus Christ.

We didn't ask God for children with special challenges, and when he gave them to us, we weren't sure what to expect. We were afraid. Parenting these children is hard. Parenting any child is hard.

But nine years ago, when my wife and I married, we asked that God would make us saints. We asked that we would be like a stained-glass window—that the light of His love would be filtered, beautifully, through our lives. We are not saints. Neither are our children. But the love of God filters through their lives. God's love, in their lives, is beautiful. And they have transformed our hearts.

J.D. Flynn is a canon lawyer and serves as the Special Assistant to Bishop James Conley in the Diocese of Lincoln. He writes and speaks on issues related to canon law, evangelization, human rights and human dignity, and disabilities. He lives in Nebraska with his patient, beautiful, and funny wife Kate, their two children, two old dogs, and a few scraggly flocks of chickens and ducks.

7

EMBRACING THE
DIFFERENCES

*It is to those who have the most need of us that
we ought to show our love more especially.*
— St. Francis de Sales —

My oldest son Alex who struggles with high-functioning autism has special needs, but I am most grateful that he is my *special child* and a blessing in our lives.

He is different, but different is not bad. It just means that the dreams we may have had for our child and the life he will lead have been altered. God has a different plan for our son and we know that blessings will come from his life. He is a special child of God and God loves him for who he is. My wife and I trust he was given to us for a reason, and we have already seen how blessed our lives are because he is our son.

As you reflect on your personal situation and the impact of having a child or children with special needs, please remember that God gave you and your wife a precious gift. As I've shared, we can't reject God's creation and wish we had a better version of His gift to us. I know many dads who in moments of candid dialogue express sadness or even bitterness that their child would not be the football hero, captain of the swim team, or a host of fantasies that we men tend to have for our children. I experienced something like this myself with Alex, but I learned over the years to celebrate what he did do well. I love his incredible memory and that he routinely beats me in Trivial Pursuit. His knowledge and enjoyment of music are a wonder as is his knowledge of the Catholic faith. He won't live out my sports dreams and I could care less. I want him to know, love, and serve God. I desire Alex's happiness. I want him to be as self-sufficient as possible. I want everyone he encounters to love and encourage him. I hope he will be able to contribute his gifts to the world. Over the years, I have simply come to embrace his differences and see them as blessings.

Other Voices

MONSIGNOR JOHN J. ENZLER

Monsignor John J. Enzler, the president and CEO of Catholic Charities of the Archdiocese of Washington, has worked extensively for many years with families who have children with special needs, and he has helpful insight into these families and the special role of the father.

Growing up in a family of thirteen children, my dad and mom were able to endure the ups and downs that come with raising children. Some of us were smarter than others, some better athletes or musicians, some more industrious, others always late, some dreamers, some doers, some more serious, and some more mischievous. Our parents taught us about love without exception. While we may have been different, Mom and Dad's love for us was equal in all regards. For me, the best part of growing up with so many siblings was coming to realize how important it was to me to live up to my mom and dad's expectations, always doing the best I could, confident that is all they ever expected.

In college, I spent many a weekend sharing activities and fun times with young people with developmental differences. That special population gave me far more than I gave to them. Since my ordination forty-one years ago, I have had the opportunity to be involved with numerous parishes. As a priest I've had a great affinity for those with developmental differences. At each parish I've been assigned I've tried to make sure that the community looks for ways to involve families who have children with developmental differences. I always enjoy seeing the beauty in their eyes and the smiles that are readily shared. These special people make my day better and remind me so clearly of God's love.

When I see families who share their love with a child with intellectual differences, I am aware of both the struggle and the beauty of raising a child with special needs. Sometimes I see a family in pain, struggling with the fact that one of their children has developmental issues that are difficult to navigate for the entire family. My heart goes out to those who seem to be overwhelmed by their daily struggles. The love is evident but the weariness and even sadness are difficult to watch. At other times, I see the same type of struggles but I am inspired by the depth of love, acceptance, and care so beautifully shared with a young person who the world might see through different eyes.

A little over two years ago I attended a funeral of a young boy who died after many years of physical and intellectual struggles. He and his dad had been so close, going on weekly bike rides, spending time watching sporting events, and many road trips in the family car. The fifteen-year-old son contracted an infection and after about ten days in the hospital and visits from many priests, he wasn't able to recover and passed away. His father gave the eulogy and simply said: "Today I am burying my best friend." His words were poignant, heartfelt, and even startling to all of us who knew of his love. That one sentence summed up what it means to be a father and how it is that a dad could look past physical and intellectual differences and only see love, companionship, and joy.

It takes a special man to be a great father to any child. These gifts, given by God, are such a blessing to one's spouse and to the children. It takes a really special father to see beyond a disability. He makes no judgment about his children's successes and flaws. It is a beautiful sight indeed.

So, I will always have a soft place in my heart, not only for the children but also for their siblings and their parents. These special families speak to me of God and allow me to get a glimpse of God's goodness and love for us. Fathers who love their children in such a special way, no matter what the struggles may be, always remind me of our God who loves us in exactly the same way, never worrying about out flaws, but rather just wanting us to live to the fullness of all we can be.

MAGGIE ROUSSEAU, M.ED.

Maggie Rousseau, M.Ed. is the director of the Disabilities Ministry for the Archdiocese of Atlanta, a culturally diverse archdiocese.

Maggie, in your role as director of the Disability Ministry with the Archdiocese of Atlanta, you work with countless Catholic families who have children with special needs. What are the biggest challenges these families face? What are you seeing?

The Catholic community in the Archdiocese of Atlanta is very diverse. Recent surveys indicate that over half the Catholics in the archdiocese are from other countries and cultures outside the United States. But those of us in the disability world know that disability does not discriminate. It is cross-cultural, affecting every culture and socio-economic classification. Although culturally different, many challenges for Catholic families living with disabilities in the Archdiocese of Atlanta are shared.

They are all living with heavy hearts; they all experience unwelcoming attitudes across environments; they all have medical concerns; they are all initially uneducated about their child's disability; they all worry about the education of their child and their child's future; they are all often unaware of resources; many are economically disadvantaged and struggle to cover basic necessities. And many do not know that a child with a disability can still participate fully in the Catholic Church.

Our multicultural families also face other barriers. They are more isolated, because of both cultural norms and circumstance. Many cultures believe that having a disability is something that is bad or shameful. Families pull away from their communities—and live in a type of sheltering-in place. They are slow to trust others outside their cultural network. Parents may lack the educational background to understand complicated medical issues. And they may come from a culture where it is unacceptable to ask questions of a superior, viewing a teacher or physician superior to themselves in regard to the care of their child. Often, cultural norms dictate how a person will parent, even though the cultural norms of their new home country allow and even expect more participation in decision-making.

These challenges are felt very strongly in our parishes. Parishes want to open doors and want to be welcoming to all, yet many parishes need more education about living with disabilities in an effort to serve all families with love.

With regard to fathers in these families, what role do they play in the "thriving" families? What do they do which is *different* from the

> men in families where they might not be as en-
> gaged as husbands and fathers?

My son Christopher was a very simple little fellow with a very difficult medical diagnosis. He lived, laughed, and loved with such enthusiasm! And he thrived because both my husband Scott and I were involved in his life. Hearing that your child has a terminal illness is horrific. Your heart is filled with such sadness. Finding and feeling joy, which will now be forever veiled by such sadness, is a challenge.

The families thriving are joyful families. They are loving families. And often Dad is the source of that joy and love. Everyone is all smiles when Dad comes in after a long day at work. Excited to be home, a father's positive energy changes the mood, his smile the sun that warms the house. Christopher absorbed that energy every time he was greeted by his daddy. And as tired as Scott was after working fourteen and sixteen hours a day, Tim, Chris, and Katie were never ignored. Scott embraced us all with enthusiasm and joy. His laugh was and still is the loudest in our house. This was very difficult for him. It distressed him that Chris was so fragile and that my life was difficult. He was worried for Tim and Katie. But he never showed it.

Many men are not good at sharing emotions, and the numerous emotions involved in parenting a child with disabilities can be overwhelming. Sadness is probably the emotion felt most. Sadness is not something you can share with others. It is personal and private, and you cannot help someone else overcome their sadness. The families I know where fathers choose to be absent are often missing joy. Rather than happy smiles and laughter, exhaustion and sadness fill the air. The environment becomes suffocating, so much so that families fall apart.

I have often felt that disappointment leads to resentment and that resentment leads to hate. Hateful relationships are hurtful relationships. Homes without sunshine struggle to thrive.

> If you could offer a candid "checklist for dads" of behaviors and ideas to help them more fully support their wives, accept and engage with their child (or children) with special needs, and be the leader in their families, what would you suggest?

- Get engaged with your family and stay engaged. If you find yourself withdrawing (working too much, avoiding home), refocus!

- Understand your child's disability. Educate yourself and ask questions for clarification. Understand treatment options for your child. Learn therapy techniques and do them with your child.

- Focus on your child's strengths. *Every* child has abilities. Focus on the abilities, not the disabilities.

- Be part of the decision-making process: attend doctor/therapy appointments; attend IEP meetings; meet with teachers and therapists; be an expert on your child with your wife!

- Participate in the lives of your other children. Often a child with a disability consumes Mom and Dad's energy and time. Remember your other children love and need you too.

- Make it a priority to tighten bonds with a faith community. Having a child with a disability either makes or breaks your faith. Your faith can be your strength. Choose faith!

- Stay engaged with friends and family. Your friends and family love you. Let them become your support system.

- Make time for your wife. Remember why you fell in love and grow from there.

- Feel the love that surrounds you. Remember God is love! You are loved! You are not alone!

8
OUR OWN UNIQUE CROSSES
Greg Willits

*On the Way of the Cross, you see, my children,
only the first step is painful. Our greatest cross is
the fear of crosses. . . . We have not the courage to
carry our cross, and we are very much mistaken;
for, whatever we do, the cross holds us tight—we
cannot escape from it. What, then, have we to
lose? Why not love our crosses, and make use of
them to take us to heaven?*
— St. Jean Marie Baptiste Vianney —

Filling three hours of radio with interesting content five days a week is not the easiest thing to do. Surprisingly, the talking part is simple. It's the pounding through countless hours of crafting thought-provoking and entertaining show prep that encompasses the most time and hard work.

When my wife and I did this as our full-time jobs from 2008 to 2012, nearly 100 percent of the content came directly from our everyday conversations about our daily life circumstances—grocery shopping, juggling five kids, trying to get those kids involved in their faith—combined with equal doses of current news events, pop culture, and ample helpings of catechesis tossed in to glue it all together. Because of the extensive time commitment show prep required, it was always a huge relief when a unique book happened our way that promised a talkative author who could appear as a guest on our program.

Therefore, having two boys diagnosed at an early age with high-functioning autism, when a new book showed up in our mailbox from an author with multiple autistic daughters, we jumped at the opportunity to have her on the program.

For us, autism manifested itself in our oldest son, Sam, as Asperger's syndrome and its characteristic deep fixations with anything from watching documentaries about locomotives to going through countless reams of paper and spools of tape in efforts to construct massive 3-D models of the Titanic, every Star Wars weapon ever created, and full body armor. Yes, all out of paper and tape.

For our third son, Ben, also diagnosed with high-functioning (but non-Aspergerian) autism, the traits were most evident in his first four years with crying fits and regular meltdowns, but even these evened out considerably in later years. For example, on Thanksgiving Day in 2003, Ben was just nineteen months old, and dinner was being placed on the table for my parents, as well as my wife's parents and her brother's family. Ben, for no apparent reason, simply lost it. Screaming uncontrollably, flailing his body madly, nothing would console him.

In my insecurity, I worried my parents saw my wife and I as failures. Why couldn't we control their grandson? Why couldn't we discipline him into submission? But this wasn't just a temper tantrum that could be fixed with a time out. This was a flat-out freak-out and something had to be done to stop it.

Trying to save Thanksgiving, I took Ben and hauled him back to the far side of the house, going through our bedroom, into the bathroom, and finally closing the two of us behind the door of our closet. I sat on the floor and clutched each of Ben's wrists in my hands and crossed his arms over his chest. With him on my lap, I curled my own legs over his to keep them from kicking.

Ben kept screaming, and screaming, and screaming. My ears rang from the scream that reached into my brain and down into my chest where the screams clutched and tensed everything within me. I had no doubt our entire family could still hear the racket from the opposite end of our home, and when Jennifer came in to relieve me nearly forty-five minutes later, Ben was still screaming, snot and tears covering his bright red face.

I walked out of the closet and my mother was washing dishes. Everyone else had already left. Thanksgiving was over, the meal we'd spent hours preparing was now nothing but a plate of leftovers waiting for me on the counter, covered with a shield of plastic wrap.

That was the same year we first attempted homeschooling, with my wife taking the lead. Every day when she tried to lead our oldest son Sam through his kindergarten and then first grade lessons, Ben screamed, loudly and for hours and hours nonstop, just as he had on Thanksgiving.

Sam covered his ears and would scream in reply. He was struggling to read, to write, and especially to do the most basic math. His entire homeschool day played out to the background music of Ben's incessant screaming and crying from first light to lights out.

Near the end of Sam's first grade year we hired a consultant to provide an educational evaluation, and it was the consultant who first recommended we take Sam in for testing. Soon after he tested positively on the autism spectrum with Asperger's syndrome, Ben was also diagnosed due to his more classic symptoms of hypersensitivity to noise, light, and other sensations, along with other factors. Upon learning the diagnosis, we were sad about the challenges we knew would be ahead of us, yet in many ways we were simply relieved to know that our children acted the way they did simply because of the way God made them, and not because of terrible parenting on our part.

To my wife and me, autism became not so much an adversity to overcome as much as it was something that was at the core of our children, ingrained in their personalities and infused in their very beings. That's not to say that autism was the center of their lives (or ours), but rather that autism simply carved two of our five children into the wonderful creations they are. From my albeit simplistic worldview, I lived under the naive assumption that other parents of autistic kids had also accepted their children as is. I never followed the group of advocates who insisted that vaccinations caused autism, or even that a cure for autism could be found. I was more focused on just accepting the way my children are, and assuming that's the way they'd always be. To me, the idea of a cure would be equivalent to completely transforming the personalities our children had developed (and we'd grown to love) into something (or someone) entirely different.

By the time the author with multiple autistic daughters was on our show, my wife and I had actually developed an appreciation for the unique characteristics our sons with autism demonstrate. In fact, I couldn't imagine Sam and Ben *without* some sort of autistic characteristics. I enjoyed sitting on the couch with them on Saturday mornings with a cup of coffee in my hand, watching documentaries about highly technical engineering concepts. As someone with an artistic bent, I was always proud of the next fanciful creation my son would manufacture out of random things left lying around the house.

Unfortunately, one downside of a daily radio show that features a new author nearly every day is that it is impossible to actually read every word of every page of every book that landed my way. Thus, despite my excitement for the content of this particular book (gleaned mostly from the jacket cover and the enclosed marketing materials sent from the publisher), I didn't really fully grasp the wide difference in autism diagnoses between the author's children and my own.

For the author, autism manifested in her daughters more severely, forcing the need for rehabilitation services and a much wider support network. This was never necessary for us. Her children required an in-school assistant to help her kids through their classes. Our children would never need such services. She was an anti-vaccine advocate. I never thought twice about vaccines or the hope of a cure.

In other words, her life was much harder than mine as a result of the severity of autism in her children.

Therefore, in the midst of our interview (which was thankfully conducted over the phone, otherwise I think the author would have punched me for my next question) I was taken completely off guard when I asked, "If a cure for autism was discovered, wouldn't you *miss* some parts of your child's personality that was caused by autism?"

In retrospect, this was a presumptuous and ignorant question to ask. But for me, I'd miss the extreme creativity of my oldest son that I believe exists in part because of his Asperger's. I'd miss my other son's sweetness and care that comes from the innocence of his autism. This was my mindset when I asked that question, which also explains why I was so taken aback at the author's angry reply, and why I felt so horrible when, just hours later, I discovered she'd even blogged about my idiocy on her website.

That author interview, and her reaction afterward, has stuck with me for years in ways that hundreds of other interviews haven't.

For one, I learned a valuable lesson about not making assumptions about the experiences and emotions of parents of other special needs kids. Your kid is your kid. Your challenges are your challenges. While there are always commonalities, it is not fair to compare your child to someone else's. Your child is a unique, special, and loved child of God, no matter what disabilities your child may or may not possess.

Secondly, it emphasized the need for the already existing term, "autism spectrum," which truly covers a huge range of conditions and challenges, some harder than others.

Thirdly, the interview made me realize how much my wife and I have been blessed by the uniqueness and, honestly, the overall mildness of the diagnosis for the two of our five children that fall on the spectrum.

For us, while there have indeed been some difficulties, challenges, and inconveniences associated with the diagnosis our children received so many years ago, I have a hard time not focusing more on the unique traits. Which, for me, as someone who struggles to balance the fine line between pessimism and realism, is not an easy thing.

But in those early years, long before that radio interview, there was something intriguing about our children having such fierce and intense fascinations with things like trains.

As our boys have grown older (as I write this, Sam is now seventeen and Ben is almost thirteen), they've mellowed greatly with age. Also, as they've grown, so too has greater awareness of the autism spectrum in our society. It comforts us to know we're not alone, that our kids aren't outcasts.

Despite their occasional quirkiness, as Sam approaches college age I sometimes wonder if his original diagnosis was even accurate. As he approaches young adulthood, Sam now shows interest in girls, has a part-time job at a sandwich shop, and not only overcame his earlier adversity to reading and writing but has developed into an artist and creative writer who hopes to go to college to study for a career in graphic design. I imagine in the next few years we'll see a similar blossoming of Ben, just as I expect a transformation in all of our children.

As for me, I've changed, too. I can't say that it was just my children's autism that changed me, though. It was just my kids through and through. All of my children have challenged me, surprised me, let me down, and lifted me up. That's why kids are such a blessing from God.

As my kids get older, I find myself regularly referring to Romans 5:3–5, which reminds us to "Rejoice in our sufferings, knowing that suffering produces endurance, and endurance produces character, and character produces hope, and hope does not disappoint us, because God's love has been poured into our hearts through the Holy Spirit who has been given to us."

This is important to remember. God gives each of us our own unique crosses, each weighing exactly as much as God gives us the capacity to handle. And these crosses are not punishments, but opportunities to grow stronger, to develop richer characters, and through that, especially in raising our children, to continually grow in greater love and deeper hope in the God who loves us just as He made us.

Greg Willits is the author of The New Evangelization and You: Be Not Afraid *and co-author of* The Catholics Next Door: Adventures in Imperfect Living. *He's an award winning radio, television, and podcast creator who has been married to his best friend, Jennifer, since 1995. Together they have five kids here on earth and several in heaven. You can find him online at www. gregwillits.com and www.gregandjennifer.com.*

9

FAITHFUL, ENGAGED, AND LEADING

Nothing is more honorable or more manly than
a father's love—day in and day out—for a child
who is 'imperfect' in the eyes of the world, but
infinitely beautiful and precious in the eyes of God.
— Archbishop Charles J.Chaput, O.F.M. Cap. —

Dads, ours is a great responsibility that goes well beyond the focus of this book and the special children with challenges who are in our care. Our vocation is to get our families (and everyone else) to heaven. Our wives and all of our children need and deserve our love, time, and support. How do we balance it all?

As I said earlier, during my prayer time I often reflect on the example of St. Joseph who is the patron saint of fathers and the best role model we can follow. What can I learn from this great saint? I'm not the expert, but it seems that if I follow the example of St. Joseph I have my priorities straight with Christ first, family second, and work third. A father who emulates St. Joseph spends *quality* time with his family, not just time. This man is a role model to his family in living out his Catholic faith and being the light of Christ to others. This father has joy in his heart and is a man of prayer. This Catholic dad honors and loves his wife and lifts up the Sacrament of Marriage in the eyes of his children as something special and sacred. He is willing to go all the way for her and not just meet her half way. He is fully engaged and the leader of his family. He sees his child (or children) with special needs as a true blessing in his life.

You know what, dads? Sometimes, you and I simply have to try harder. We have to give our best, even when we don't feel like it or we feel overwhelmed. We have to sacrifice some work time, fun time, down time, and me time for the sake of our families. My father once told me that it was a privilege to work hard and sacrifice for the benefit of our family, and I have never forgotten those words. I also learned through my parents and my Catholic faith to view my family, especially my son with special needs, as a blessing for which I should be extremely grateful.

As I have done throughout *Special Children, Blessed Fathers*, I was eager to get the perspectives of others for this chapter. I reached out to the Grieg family and first interviewed their twenty-four-year old daughter Kristen. My second interview was with Patti Grieg, the mother of the family. We discussed seventeen-year-old Marie Claire, who has Down syndrome, and the role of the father Dale Grieg in making their family dynamic work.

Other Voices

KRISTEN GRIEG

As the sibling of a child with Down syndrome, what has life been like in your family?

Pretty easy. Dad has always been able to provide for our family and we received a great education. Having a sibling with Down syndrome hasn't made my life any easier or harder. If anything, my relationship with my other sister without Down syndrome has made my life more difficult because we don't get along very well sometimes. I'm the oldest, so I have always played more of a motherly role toward my sisters, especially Mary Claire. Her disability became most noticeable to me in middle school, and I was more sympathetic and compassionate towards other students with disabilities, which raised questions from my classmates. Some people didn't understand why I would sit with the special needs girl at lunch, but I have always been more aware and sensitive to people with special needs. It is easy to be Mary Claire's sister because she is usually very pleasant and amiable. I know people with a sibling with a much more severe case of

Down syndrome and their response would likely be much different than mine.

What are your best memories of the role your father has played in helping the family stay on track?

We always went to Mass as a family, including when we went on vacation. I think that going to Mass on vacation showed us that as Catholics, we don't take a break from worshiping Christ just because we are away from our home church. It reinforced the universality of the Church to me. Dad has faithfully attended Eucharistic adoration for over ten years I believe, and that has been a strong testament to the strength of his faith. I read the quote that the best thing a father can do for his daughters is to love their mother, and that has always been true in our family. We never questioned if Dad was coming home after a business trip or if he might one day leave us. That was never a possibility in my mind growing up. He had a reliable father and I am sure that his father's example also played a role in his development as a dad. Dad would wear a scapular and usually have a rosary nearby. I didn't see him pray it often, which doesn't mean that he didn't pray the Rosary, but I do remember seeing his rosary out around the house or sitting on his dresser. Dad was also a good participant at Mass. He has been a greeter and a Eucharistic minister, and he would always say the prayers and sing out loud. A lot of men are too proud to sing at Mass. That sets a bad example for their kids, like they are too cool to participate in church. I'm glad my dad sings at Mass.

> Can you describe your parent's marriage
> and how that has impacted your family over
> the years?

They have set a good example for my sister and me of what a successful marriage looks like. We prayed the Rosary several times together as a family, and Mom and Dad would always lead us in prayer on long road trips. Seeing the family pray the Rosary around my dying grandmother was a very comforting sight and also reinforced our faith.

PATTI GRIEG, THE MOTHER OF KRISTEN

> Patti, could you share a little about your daugh-
> ter and her diagnosis?

Mary Claire is currently seventeen years old. I elected not to have any type of prenatal testing, and so her diagnosis of Down syndrome at birth was a complete surprise. In addition, she had a major heart defect, which can be common for these children. I left the hospital without our new baby. That was an awful feeling. Mary Claire underwent emergency heart surgery at about four weeks, and her prognosis for survival was very low. Obviously, she pulled through! Her second heart repair took place approximately four months afterward. We spent years going to therapies (speech, occupational, physical, hippotherapy) and doctors. Mary Claire has no medical restrictions and a clean bill of health. Modern medicine!

Down syndrome occurs in approximately one of every 600-800 births. There is no hereditary factor. They are able to determine which parent gave the extra chromosome, but this was not something we were interested in pursuing. It is most common, however, that the mother passes along the extra chromosome.

Mary Claire attended special needs pre-school in the public school system. She then went to her homeschool for elementary and was mainstreamed most of the day. She went to middle school for two years and then I homeschooled her for two years. She is currently a junior in our high school in a Mild Intellectually delayed classroom.

Presently, Mary Claire works at a local restaurant for two mornings a week. Her boss says she is her best hire! She also loves dance and has participated in class with typical students as well as for girls with Down syndrome. Her dance company has been selected to go to Disney World this summer for a workshop and performance. Mary Claire also is an altar server and received the "Altar Server of the Year award" from the Knights of Columbus.

How has she been a blessing in your lives?

As a parent of a child with a disability, I've always said that the highs are high and the lows are low. You experience lows in life you think you can never overcome, but you do. However, the joys you will experience are greater than the lows. I think these highs are even almost a greater experience than those of our typical children, because of the obstacles and difficulties a special needs child must overcome.

We certainly have learned about what's important in life and having the right priorities. You don't sweat so much of the small stuff!

We have had experiences and met people we would have otherwise never known or encountered. We have experienced goodness that we otherwise would not have known. The special needs child teaches empathy, kindness, and patience to all of us. Siblings also benefit enormously.

When Mary Claire was born, we only had one person who said, "Congratulations." People talk about having a "healthy baby." Of course, we all wish for healthy children, but that does not make them 'perfect.' I do not have to label her as high or low functioning. In God's eyes, my child is perfect.

What has been the most important thing Dale has done for your family as a Catholic husband and father?

When Mary Claire had her heart surgeries, we were exposed to a world in the hospital we never knew. Many of the patients came from low income/uneducated homes. These mothers may not have received proper prenatal care and the children were very sick. Often, only a mother was in the picture and the nurses said it's not unusual if a father isn't involved. Up to this point I took for granted that my husband would be present. I guess I expected nothing less, when in reality we both were very fortunate.

I can't imagine having to have gone through all the difficulties on my own. Dale was a source of strength throughout and I believe much of this was due to his faith. Immediately after the birth, Dale's first thought was to call the priest to come and bless Mary Claire.

One evening I was having a particularly difficult time after the birth and broke down. I asked Dale, "What are we going to do?" Without hesitation Dale calmly said, "She's our daughter." At that moment I truly felt the Holy Spirit was working through Dale, and I had a sense of peace and the strength to move forward. Sounds simple, but the moment seemed very powerful and one I've never forgotten.

I hope these examples help explain the importance of Dale's faith and his trust in God. His faith is what gives him the foundation and strength to be my husband and the father of our family. He continues to be an example to me and our daughters of his faithfulness and the importance of prayer.

If Dale had neglected his vocation as a Catholic husband and father and been disengaged, how might things have turned out for all of you?

As stated above, many families do not stay intact once a child with a disability comes into the family. Even later, stresses can fracture both the marriage and the family, and divorce occurs. If Dale had neglected his faith, that could have been us. If anything, he has grown in his faith since the birth of Mary Claire. It has drawn him closer to God. Again, that's not something to take for granted. His continuing to be active at church and leading a prayerful life is so important. It's like the oil for your car, it keeps things in good working order!

If you could sit down with a family that has received the diagnosis of Down syndrome for an expected child, what would you like to say to them? Especially to the father?

Being a parent is not easy. But being a parent of a child with special needs is a more difficult path (sometimes lonely), one which we would sometimes like to exit. However, your family will receive many graces and blessings for which they have no comprehension. Mary Claire is a kind, sensitive, engaging, funny, and loving daughter, made perfect in His eyes. Down syndrome is only part of who she is.

I would say to the father: you are going to need your Catholic faith and church community to be a good husband and father. Continue to nurture your faith through the sacraments, prayer, and Mass.

10

A DIFFERENT LIFE
Matthew Warner

*For the LORD gives wisdom; from his mouth come
knowledge and understanding; he stores up sound
wisdom for the upright; he is a shield to those who
walk in integrity, guarding the paths of justice and
preserving the way of his saints. Then you will
understand righteousness and justice and equity,
every good path.*
— Proverbs 2:6–9 —

Many decisions in life are made based simply on what everyone else is doing. We subconsciously conform to the norm or what we think we're supposed to do, whether it's the careers we pursue, the lifestyle we are working toward, or simply the kinds of things we do on a Saturday night or a Sunday morning. But every once in a while we get nudged in a different direction. We have some kind of unexpected event that forces upon us a new perspective and a different kind of life.

For our family, that nudge came one otherwise normal November day four years ago.

She was wrapped in a blanket, looking up at us through tiny, half-moon eyes. My wife cried and I stood steady as we listened to the neonatologist on staff tell us—only minutes after she was born—that she had Down syndrome. And everything that meant.

We knew we loved our daughter regardless of any diagnosis, but it was the sudden onset of uncertainty that shocked us most. What did all this mean? For her life? For our life? For our other children? This wasn't the child we had planned for or expected.

The doctor said it meant she had an extra chromosome. That she had an increased risk of heart defects, childhood leukemia, thyroid conditions, and a host of other health problems that we needed to test for right away. He said she would have low muscle tone, learning delays, and many other unique challenges in life.

My head was whizzing and overwhelmed, but I was hyperfocused. We had a wonderful outpouring of emotional support at that time, but I was focused on the task at hand: taking care of our daughter. Those first few days were spent learning a lot about numerous medical tests and conditions, asking continuous questions and googling everything "Down syndrome" until the wee hours of the morning.

I rushed to fill that sudden onset of uncertainty with the certainty of every fact I could find. We analyzed and worried over every challenge our daughter may potentially experience throughout the course of her entire life as a result of this particular condition—all before she even left the hospital. What challenges will she face? What will high school be like for her? Will she ever be able to move out or get married? What about her education? What about our other children? Will she need special therapy and what kind? Immediately her entire life, every possible path it could take, and anything it could possibly mean for our family was racing through our heads. Life was going to be different—but how different?

It's the kind of mental exercise that would overwhelm any father, whether his child has special needs or not. But, of course, I had to make sure she got what she needed.

Those first months were tough. My wife and I had been asleep at the wheel, nudged off the wide road, and awoke to find ourselves down the road less traveled. Naturally, it took some time to figure out what had just happened to us. And we were desperate to cure the uncertainty of this "different kind of life" that had been thrust upon us. I needed to regain firm control of the plan for our life.

But as I searched and searched to learn more about Kate's special needs, I gradually realized that God was actually teaching me about my own. And the more I worked to provide for her needs, the more God was providing for mine. Eventually it became clear to me that this unexpected adventure was not so much about how much Kate needed from the world, but how much the world needed her.

Many of us spend our days trying to make life easier. We imagine that having a lot of success—extra money and influence, a nice house, the ideal family, and plenty of free time for pursuing hobbies and career interests—will make for an easier, happier life.

Deep down we know it's not true. Not only does every bit of conventional wisdom expose this lie, but we also see it played out every day as we learn of the unhappiness of the rich. Yet we still insist on learning it the hard way ourselves, often wasting our lives pursuing this "easier life."

I'm one of the lucky ones, though. Having a child with special needs is like a secret shortcut. When you have somebody who needs you a little differently, you have much less interest and energy to waste on lesser pursuits. Of course, having any children at all does this in its own beautiful way. But having a child that nudges us out of the norm and demands our attention in a different way has been a great gift.

There is no sugar-coating the extra challenges that may come with having a child with special needs. But, for us, while some things are a little harder, the most important things in life are actually easier. It has joyfully compelled us to live the life of service to which we were already called. And when you begin to live in this way—with less room for your own selfish ambitions—it's easier to see the simple and miraculous life God planned for you.

Mother Teresa said, "The fruit of service is peace." Well, we've learned that all the unexpected trials of life are not really burdens at all, but opportunities to serve. They are the path to peace.

And truly, we've found Kate is just like any of our other kids—each with their own unique set of strengths and challenges, talents, and personality traits. Having a child with Down syndrome, in itself, has been such a joyful experience for us and has helped us to appreciate the individuality of all of our children on a different level.

Our faith was certainly tested through all of this. We were compelled to remember that God knows what He's doing, even when we don't. That His plan is good even when we don't understand it. It's *especially* when we don't understand His plan, we have found, that He seems to be working on us most, and in ways we didn't even know needed working on.

Suddenly and unexpectedly we had to question the plans for our life that we had held for so long. *Is this really what God wants for our life? Or is this just what we want? Is it His plan? Or our plan? And have we ever really been open to anything different?* Kate inspired us to think differently about everything in life. We were nudged out of our comfort zone, and since it seemed we'd already be doing things a little differently anyway, we were open to consider other ways we should be living differently, too.

In the years following Kate's birth, we've spent energy on organizing priorities and living with purpose. We moved closer to family. We bought acreage to spend more time outdoors. We're homeschooling, starting a vegetable garden, minimizing screen time and devices, praying daily as a family, and spending more time singing, dancing, and playing together.

Making room for these changes was difficult. And the specific changes will vary for every family, of course. But the point was that they were discerned, deliberate, and, yes, often different than what we had planned.

I used to think that being a good father meant making sure I was doing enough for my children and my marriage, leaving the rest of my time for my own pursuits. Then I realized what an uninspiring and boring way that is to live life. Now, instead, I'm energized by the constant exploration of ways that I can give still more to each member of my family. That makes each day a new, exciting, and fulfilling challenge.

Kate's birth unveiled a different path for us that we never knew existed—and now we rejoice in the opportunity and adventure of the road less traveled.

As a father, I am a primary instrument God uses to lead my children to Him. I play a pivotal and active role in helping them have a "successful" life. But what makes for a successful life anyway? Kate helped me rethink the answer to this essential question, and she changed the way I view not just her life but the lives of all my children, my wife, and myself.

After all, we're not just trying to produce a bunch of self-dependent cogs in a wheel, forming productive citizens who "pull their own weight." Don't get me wrong. The pursuit of excellence is a good thing, a very Catholic thing, and productivity is a good and necessary thing. But that's not the end goal. That's not the measure of a meaningful life. To maximize our productivity on this planet is not our purpose; yet, how often do the metrics we use in forming our children communicate precisely this message?

The end goal is not that our kids go out and produce heaps of things, make lots of money, receive many accolades, and have predictable, well-planned, responsible lives . . . but that they go out and become saints. That they go out and love others and, in turn, create more saints.

Americans worry about why one state's math scores are higher than another's. At home we put our kids through a heck of a lot (and we sacrifice a lot) to make sure they pass their tests, know how to read and write, and can recite their multiplication tables. Many parents even stress about whether their children are able to do certain things at the right age, or are a year ahead or behind the other kids.

It always feels like there's so much *more* we could be doing for our children: more enrichment activities, more crafts, more sports, more opportunities for them to grow, more experiences to develop their little brains so they can be more successful. Naturally, those pressures can be even stronger for parents of a child with special needs: more therapies, more early intervention, more and more and more. . . .

All of that is important, but it's nowhere near as important as a lot of other things in life that deserve far more attention.

When Kate (or any of my children for that matter) are grown, it won't really matter if she got through seventh grade on time. It won't matter how far she could kick a soccer ball. It won't really matter much if she's done all the things a typical young lady might do, although I know she'll do many of them.

There are so many more important metrics to go by to help our kids live meaningful lives, such as:

- **Are they humble?** Not to think less of themselves, but to think of themselves less.

- **Do they know how to be loved?** Are they humble and secure enough to be vulnerable?

- **Are they at peace?** Do they know who they are?

- **Are they filled with joy?** Do they live with a hope that transcends this short life?

- **Do they know they are small?** That the world is not about them.

- **Do they know they are giants?** That, to somebody, they mean the whole world.

- **Are they adventurous?** Are they willing to embrace a faith that will take them beyond the prison of their own limits?

- **Are they imaginative?** Can they see that the best parts of life cannot be measured or touched?

- **Do they embrace the moment?** Do they know the present moment is the only moment they'll ever have?

- **Are they virtuous?** Do they aspire to the best parts of their nature?

- **Do they know how to give generously?** Because to give of yourself is the only way to find yourself.

- **Do they know how to love?** Because this is what they were made to do. (And because I've shown them by loving them every day unconditionally and by introducing them to God who loves them perfectly).

This is what "success" looks like. This is what I'd like my kids to "want to be when they grow up." The classes and the homework and the tests and the therapies and the career path are all a bonus. You can earn a college degree or become a CEO without learning far more important life lessons. If I measure Kate's life by the most important metrics, ironically she's actually way ahead of the curve. And the truth is, she's already taught me more about these things than I'll ever teach her.

When you look at Kate, you can't help but instantaneously become a better person. She makes you quickly forget about the many shallow, less important distractions in life. And not because you're consumed by her needs, but because you're taken in and swept away by her radiant beauty and joy—a joy that has little to do with the frivolities of life and everything to do with authentic love and purpose.

I have a special need. Our family has a special need. The world has a special need. And her name is Kate.

Matthew Warner is the founder of Flocknote.com, a blessed husband and a grateful father trying his best to balance it all. He's also a prolific blogger, contributor to the book The Church and New Media, *and author of* TheRadicalLife.org. *Matt has a bachelor of science in electrical engineering from Texas A&M and a master of business administration in entrepreneurship. He and his family hang their hats in Texas.*

11

For Better or Worse

*To maintain a joyful family requires much from
both the parents and the children. Each member of
the family has to become, in a special way,
the servant of the others.*
— Pope St. John Paul II —

Since our son was diagnosed with autism in 1999, my wife and I have worked very hard to maintain as normal a family life as possible. We are focused on helping our oldest son live an independent life and we feel that treating him like his younger brother, giving him responsibilities around the house, and pushing him to excel will help him later in life. It is not a perfect family life and we certainly have difficult days, but it works because we are committed to the family and each other. It works because we pray and our Catholic faith plays an integral part in our lives.

For a number of years I have been a Eucharistic Adoration Guardian at our parish at 5:00 a.m. every Wednesday. One of the people also responsible for that hour is Joan McCarty. I have long respected Joan and admire the great family she and her husband have raised. Her oldest son John has low-functioning autism, and I can see the love and care the entire family gives him during Mass each week. I was keen on having Joan offer her thoughts about life in her home with a child who has special needs and the role her husband plays in the family.

Other Voices

JOAN MCCARTY

My husband John and I have been married twenty-three years, and my son John (same name) is nineteen years old and the second oldest of five children. He was diagnosed with autism at two years old. He has three sisters: Alma (twenty-one), Grace (eighteen), and Agnes (fifteen). He also has a fifteen-year-old brother, Owen, who is Agnes' twin.

Having a son with a disability has not affected my marriage any more than having four other children without disabilities has affected my marriage. Or, put another way, he's just another of my kids, and kids change a married relationship. But who can determine how that change is measured or even what it is? Who can figure out which kid it is that affects the marriage most, since all kids are different and need different things?

Because John has a significant disability, everything we do has to consider John and what his possible response to . . . anything . . . would be. There are some things we don't do because John would have a very difficult time tolerating them. For example, we don't all go to the high school for the basketball games. When attending an event for one of John's sisters or his brother, we might sit farther away from other spectators so that John has less access to them. (He sometimes interacts with strangers in an inappropriate manner.) Lots of planning is required when we're going to do something as a family or if we're going to do something with John.

It just is what it is. We plan for one thing and there's usually a contingency plan. Sometimes my husband or I will take John to the car if we need to stay somewhere for a longer time. Or we just leave if it's not going well for John. Or we bring items to keep him (hopefully) busy.

My husband and I are on the same page where John is concerned. For the most part, I am the one who researches opportunities or educational and therapeutic options and I am the one who advocates for John. I may be the one who decides which option I prefer and think is best, but I always discuss it with my husband until we agree with what we're going to do.

Before we moved to Roswell, Georgia seven years ago, John had been in a very inclusive environment in his local school with his brother and two of his sisters for a couple of years. It was fabulous and John made significant progress academically and socially.

When we moved here, we found inclusive educational practices to be nonexistent. After spending some time with the local schools, I knew I couldn't send John to a school every day where he would be marginalized, isolated, and could easily be abused. My husband and I agreed that I would homeschool John. This was very difficult to do with John since it was so isolating and he was already really struggling with the move. It was very hard on me because caring for my family seemed to take all of my time—I didn't seem to have any extra. My husband understood this, and one day said to me, "I just want you to know that I know it's very hard and I am very proud of you."

My husband is a steady presence in the family fabric. He takes his responsibilities as provider seriously, and makes time to help with shuttling the kids to and from practices, attending games, etc. He cares that we eat dinner every evening as a family. He also helps me with the support John needs in his daily living activities. For years my husband took John kayaking every weekend on the Chattahoochee River because he knew how much John loved the water. (Until John got too heavy. . . . He has difficulty with the motor planning needed to paddle the kayak.) My husband's mantra concerning John, "What's not to like?"

It is helpful for one person to have the moral and physical support of a spouse or partner when someone needs extra help within the family. A good attitude about helping is critical. My husband is never grumpy about giving John support, or giving support within the family to any of our other children. While each of our children is an individual with hopes and dreams—and we acknowledge those—no one single person's needs, including John's, overrule what occurs in our family. As a unit, each person is important, but it's the sum of the units where most of our energies are focused.

That said, my children without disabilities know that John gets extra support because he needs it. They also know that everyone is going to get what they need. They know that John belongs to all of us and as such, we are all gifts to one another.

The view of and attitude toward a child and their disability is the single most important thing. My husband and I (as well as our children without disabilities) don't see John—and never did—as flawed. John is how God wants him, and we're okay with that. John just is who he is.

12
MOMMY'S LITTLE ANGEL
Bill Jones

So faith, hope, love abide, these three;
but the greatest of these is love.
— 1 Corinthians 13:13 —

On May 5, 2006, a doctor spent less than five minutes with our precious two-year-old boy before telling my wife that he "definitely has autism."

We had been so convinced that there was nothing more than typical developmental delays associated with being a boy and the first child that I didn't even go to the appointment. My wife went alone. The doctor delivered the devastating news with clinical precision offering little more than a flyer for the local autism support group. My wife and I were shocked. How could this happen to us? We knew nothing about autism, and our only reference for autism was the movie Rain Man. None of our friends had children with autism, but their kids were talking in sentences.

I immediately began researching autism on the Internet. The prognosis was not good. He would likely need a lifetime of care as very few children with autism lived independently, most did not have jobs, and there was no way to recover from it. I knew that our young family would have a tough road ahead. We felt very alone.

That night before I tucked my little boy into bed, I held him really tight, rocked him slowly, and cried. I told him that Mommy and Daddy loved him. That we'd always be there for him and would do everything we could to help him. As I was about to kiss him goodnight, I looked up and saw a sign in his room I had never noticed before. The sign showed a kind woman holding her baby with the inscription "Mommy's Little Angel." At that very moment I remembered that we were not going to be alone on this journey, and that Jesus would be there every step of the way.

I suspect that we were like many families after learning that their child had been diagnosed with autism. We began a seemingly never-ending carousel of therapy sessions, including speech therapy, occupational therapy to strengthen his hands, core body strength, and various therapies to desensitize him to all of the stimulants that were affecting his ability to interact with the world. We had him tested in every way possible, desperately searching for a way to help him. We also enrolled him in a school where he received Applied Behavior Analysis (ABA) therapy, and in the evenings we spent time with him doing floor time therapy. All of these were attempts to "fix" his autism so he could lead a "normal life." During these years of intensive therapy, we were fortunate to meet many wonderful, engaging, and special children who were also on the autism spectrum, while also getting to know their parents who were on journeys just like ours.

As Warner grew older we became involved in a ministry at our church that focused on families with special needs children. Through many outstanding hours of meetings, we were introduced to families dealing with a wide variety of disabilities. Listening to their unique stories of the struggles and the joy their special children brought to them, we learned how much richer their lives had become because of their children. We realized that while we were trying to "fix" Warner's autism, he was actually fixing us and bringing abundant life to our family.

During one meeting, a member of our group told the story of how he was concerned that his beautiful young daughter, who has Down syndrome, would be viewed by others as disruptive at Mass. After one such occasion during which she had pinched an elderly woman, the woman said that she had a son with Down syndrome who was institutionalized. She then insinuated that all of these children belonged in an institution.

My friend was deeply hurt and scheduled a meeting with a priest to discuss his daughter's place in the Church. The priest was very encouraging and told him that his daughter should sit in the first pew so she can do her job and continue to perform her important ministry!

As parents of special needs children, it can be very difficult to attend Mass as we never know when our kids will start screaming, pinch their neighbors, take their clothes off, or make an unexpected dash for the altar. While it's often challenging, and we'll sometimes have to endure stares and disapproving looks, we must allow these children to do the work that God has called them to do.

When Warner was young, we had a very difficult time getting through Mass. He would scream and cry because it was a setting that overwhelmed his senses. He also invented, tested, and mastered new and unusual ways to get out of Mass. I will never forget sitting in Mass during a quiet and reverential moment when the congregation was supposed to be deep in prayer, and Warner screamed at the top of his lungs, "My heart is full of darkness!" Warner won that round and we quietly (and quickly) exited the church. However, we were back the next week for another round!

Every Catholic parent wants their children to fully participate in the sacraments of the Church. I was concerned that Warner may have difficulty preparing for Confession and First Communion if he did not receive some accommodations. As has always been the case, Warner proved that my worries were for naught. Through the help of our priest, who specially set Warner's first confession to be in his office, Warner made it through with flying colors. Leading up to his First Communion, Warner practiced receiving the Eucharist with unconsecrated hosts so he could get used to the texture. Last year, Warner and one of his younger brothers received their First Communion together—a very special day for our family. I encourage all parents to work closely with their priests (pushing as necessary) to ensure that their children with special needs receive the sacraments.

Not unlike our other children, Warner continues to have challenges, but he meets each one of them with an unbelievably positive attitude and a quick sense of humor. He has a twinkle in his eye when talking about the things that are meaningful to him, and opens all of us to his areas of interest. One example is Civil War history. My in-laws live in a small town about an hour east of Atlanta. According to local legend, General William T. Sherman marched through the town and saved my in-laws' historical home because he thought that it was a school for girls. This particular fact brought Warner a great deal of excitement, inspiring him to read everything he could about the Civil War. Thankfully, he is in a school where they encourage students to pursue their passions, and he has now written several stories about the Civil War generals, the battles, the weapons, and the journeys made by the Union and Confederate soldiers. Five years ago, we never would have been able to get him to write a sentence, let alone a story! Now, he lectures us about the Confederate's failed attempts to defeat the Union (with whom he quickly aligned himself as they were the ultimate victors). Listening to him talk about the various nuances of the Civil War can still evoke tears in my eyes as I recall the hours of ABA therapy when he received a piece of candy for saying, "Go up." Every day I thank God for the miracle he gave me.

I often talk to parents of children who have been recently diagnosed with autism, and encourage them to be relentless advocates for their child. Due to the perspective we have gained as parents of a special needs child, my wife and I find ourselves having to be outspoken in ways we never expected. We have become advocates of insurance reform. We were forced to litigate against our local school system to ensure that Warner received an appropriate education. And we have worked for Warner to have the opportunity to receive a Catholic education.

While we have not yet obtained success in all of these efforts, we owe it to Warner and all of these special children to do everything we can to ensure that they have the same opportunities as their brothers, sisters, and friends. We strongly believe that our increased service to others has been paralleled by Warner's significant improvement over the years. The more we advocated for insurance reform, the more Warner seemed to learn at school. The more we brought parents of children with special needs together and tried to provide them with resources and connections to those with similar challenges, the more Warner was able to engage his peers. The seemingly congruent relationship between our service to others and our child's steady improvement has helped us recognize that Warner is indeed a unique gift from God.

My wife, Cammi, is Warner's biggest fan. Like many moms of special needs kids, she works tirelessly for her boys, is a patient listener, and the rock of our family. She has somehow managed to juggle the demands of raising three boys, working a full-time job as an attorney, and being a devoted friend to many. We have been married for fifteen years and I am continually in awe of how she always puts the needs of others first. We recently attended a wedding and reception in Florida where loud music was being played. Cammi noticed one family sitting far from the dance floor. They had a son wearing earplugs who was clearly on the autism spectrum. Instead of leaving this family alone, Cammi introduced herself, struck up a conversation with the boy's mother, and told her that we had a son on the autism spectrum as well. She offered him an iPhone to watch a movie, and discussed the quality of the school systems in Florida. This particular family seemed very relieved to have someone relate to them at the wedding. While they had been considering leaving early when Cammi first struck up the conversation, they were among the last to leave because they were having such a good time talking to her.

Oftentimes, just a knowing smile or kind word will completely transform the day for a family that's having a difficult time with their child. With a positive and inclusive approach, having a child with special needs can create a more connected community with love and empathy at its core.

Realizing the paramount importance of a father's presence, I have always tried to play an active role in our children's lives. My role in Warner's development has been essential in helping my over-extended wife get him to his therapy appointments, attend meetings within the school system, and be involved in autism advocacy efforts. I encourage all fathers of children with special needs to be involved with their children. They are God's gift to you and they are in your life for a purpose. Being Warner's father has made me a better father, a better husband, and a better man. I have learned to find joy in his small and big achievements, as I know how hard he has worked to get him where he is today. I also have learned humility and empathy since we began this journey believing that our child might never talk. I have also learned to appreciate and value all of the people in Warner's life who have helped him along the way. If asked today whether I would want to remove Warner's autism or change him in any way, my answer would be unequivocally: No way! Warner is the light of my life, and a light to so many others. He puts a smile on my face at times when no one else can. He has an endearing quality that affects all who meet him. If I were to "fix" his autism, it would take away the wonderful personality and beautiful soul embodied in my son.

Many people that meet Warner don't know that he has autism, but he has distinct social quirks including minimal eye contact and a tendency to focus intensely on topics that matter to him. What can't be missed in a limited conversation with him is his unbelievable memory, his quick wit, and his knack for creating humor in the most interesting ways. Warner's nickname is The Professor. This summer he participated in a Vacation Bible School and carpooled with some neighbors who knew him, but they didn't know him well. By the end of the week, the mother of the children shared with us that her daughters thought Warner was the smartest person in the world. They wondered how he could possibly know all of the facts that he has stored away in his brain. Perhaps it is because he is able to convince librarians at school to allow him to check out encyclopedias (which are not usually allowed to leave the library as they are reference books) so that he can learn more about a variety of topics.

Whatever the reason, my sincere hope for him is that he continues his education to become the zoologist, paleontologist, or some other "ologist" that he wants to be. Currently, he wants to go to college in Sydney, Australia, because there is a university that has a joint program allowing students to study both zoology and paleontology. While that is too far away for me, I will fully support him if that is where his adventure leads him.

Wherever he ends up, I know that he will inspire others to be better people. He inspires me every day. I often think back to that night I held Warner after his diagnosis and remember the moment of peace when I read the sign "Mommy's Little Angel." Indeed, God has had His hand in our journey the whole way.

At our wedding, we chose the Scripture reading from 1 Corinthians 13:13: "So faith, hope, love abide, these three; but the greatest of these is love." This verse means so much more to me now because Warner's personality, smile, and the way he lives his life has embodied that Scripture passage. He brings faith, hope, and love to all he meets, and has opened our eyes to the many blessings God has brought to our life through him.

Bill Jones is a partner at the law firm of Carlock Copeland & Stair. Bill and his wife Cammi have been married for more than fifteen years and have been blessed with three beautiful boys. Bill is committed to ensuring that every family with special needs children feels welcome at each and every facet of Catholic life: in Mass, in religious education classes, and in Catholic schools. You can find Bill online at www.linkedin.com/in/williampjones.

13

GREAT EXAMPLES

*A vocation to fatherhood is, at the best of times,
a vocation which demands unselfishness and
demands a considerable degree of trust
in Providence.*
— Monsignor Ronald Knox —
In Soft Garments

There are days when I struggle as a father. Occasionally, I lose patience with Alex and his numerous questions. Sometimes, I would rather be by myself than engage with the family because I am emotionally and physically worn out. There are times when I wonder if I can shoulder the financial responsibility that must be met for us to keep our sons in private school and pay for therapists and medications for Alex. I would love to say I have it all figured out, but I do not.

But I do have Jesus. I have my Catholic faith and the sacraments. I have the intercession of the Blessed Mother and St. Joseph and a vibrant prayer life. I have a supportive parish community and good friends. I have the love of my wife and my children who need me to be strong. All of this keeps me focused and gets me through the toughest days.

I also have great examples to follow in St. Joseph, my own father, the contributing writers in this book, and other men I have encountered over the years whose examples inspire me to be a better father, husband, and Catholic man.

When I was discerning and praying about this book, I did a great deal of research on resources for Catholic families with special needs children and stumbled upon the National Catholic Partnership on Disability (NCPD.org) in Washington, D.C. NCPD guides initiatives aimed at promoting greater participation of persons with disabilities in the Catholic Church. Jan Benton, the executive director of NCPD, frequently speaks at national and diocesan conferences and appears as a guest on national Catholic radio. She is a professed secular Franciscan and wife and mother to two adult children.

As I learned more about this wonderful organization, I felt inspired to donate the book royalties for *Special Children, Blessed Fathers* to the organization. I called Jan out of the blue and I am sure she thought I was crazy, but we eventually got to know each other and discovered our shared passion for helping and encouraging Catholic families with special needs children.

I asked Jan to share her perspectives on the examples of great fathers she has encountered over the years who have inspired her by the way they fully engaged in their vocation as fathers to their children with special needs.

Other Voices

JAN BENTON

Over the past decades in which I've been engaged in ministry with persons with disabilities in the Catholic Church, I have been blessed to know many fathers raising young and adult children with disabilities. Common among them is their love for and acceptance of their child(ren) and determination to secure all the best opportunities for them. Increasingly I am meeting grandfathers who share these same feelings and concerns for their grandchild(ren) diagnosed with a disability.

I recently attended a three-day conference in Rome sponsored by the Pontifical Council for Health Care Workers on the topic of "The Person with Autism Spectrum Disorders: Animating Hope." The most touching moment for me was during a question-and-answer period on the first afternoon when many parents asked heartfelt questions about needed services for their children. One father in particular captivated the crowd when he stated with great passion: "One thing that we all have in common is attending Mass. Couldn't our Holy Father Pope Francis ask his priests throughout the world to let our children participate in the Mass and parish life?" His longing to share his faith with his child and to feel a sense of belonging in his parish community was palpable.

Many fathers, in the course of parenting their child with a physical or intellectual disability, end up in leadership roles in both secular and faith-based groups. Some help to establish a parent support group, while others become strong advocates fighting for funding for health care and other community-based services.

In my personal life, two great fathers stand out. Neither has taken leadership roles as described above. They just lovingly raised their sons to be wonderful men. The first is my brother, Pat, whose only son Michael has an intellectual disability and diabetes. Pat is a fun-loving dad and patient teacher, always including Mike in activities such as biking and bowling. Mike and Pat do chores together, lovingly taking care of our aging mother/grandmother by carrying out mundane tasks from buying groceries for her to fun events like decorating for Christmas. They often travel together to visit family members in other states.

The second important father in my life was my late father-in-law J.C. Benton (Dad), who raised my husband, Martin, to be a loving, conscientious, and thoughtful man. Martin, diagnosed with cerebral palsy at around age two, grew up in rural Georgia in the 1950s and 60s before the enactment of the current laws that protect the rights of individuals with disabilities. Martin was raised as an integral member of the family and community, included in regular classrooms and church events. Dad worked hard at a number of jobs, determined that Martin and his siblings would attend college and have a full range of opportunities. He proudly supported Martin in his studies as a lawyer, and assisted him to move to Washington, D.C. to accept his first job with the federal government.

When Martin was hospitalized because of a psychotic episode in our first year of marriage, Dad came to assist me and provide needed moral support. Martin and I were blessed to spend a quiet afternoon with Dad just two days before he died. Dad revealed to us that when Martin was diagnosed with cerebral palsy, the family physician advised him to institutionalize him rather than try to raise him at home. Dad's response? "You'll have to take me with him." Martin was very moved and surprised to hear his father share this story, and we give thanks for his determination which has led to such a full life for Martin, me, and our two children.

BETH FOY

Beth Foy is the wife of Michael Foy, who is part of the Catholic Charities Leadership Class program of which the author was a board member.

Beth, when you think about your family life with a child with special needs, would you describe it as stressful, a blessing, or both?

Having a child with special needs is both stressful and a blessing at the same time. However, Hannah has helped us to put the stress of daily life in perspective. We no longer stress over the small stuff, like having a less-than-perfect house, and furniture that doesn't look like it was taken from the pages of a Pottery Barn catalogue, or having meals homemade from scratch for dinner every night. We prefer to spend time together as a family enjoying the outdoors over spending our week-

ends at stores. We tend to only get stressed over the big things
. . . hospitalizations, health issues, and the well-being of family
and friends.

The logistics of having a child with special needs is especially challenging for us because our older daughter, Sarah, attends
a Catholic school, but as a child with special needs Hannah is
precluded from doing the same. We often feel like our family is
split apart by this, with each of us running in different directions and our children not having the benefit of being part of a
school community together.

> How important is your husband Michael's role
> in making your family dynamic work and how
> does your Catholic faith fit into that?

Michael is essential to our family dynamic. He is often the lev-
elheaded, logical voice of reason and has the ability to work
through issues by putting the emotions aside. He is the ultimate
protector of our family in all aspects and makes sure we are well
taken care of, putting us first in the decisions that he makes.

The girls enjoy spending time with Michael and he has
made a great effort to take time for them, despite the demands
of a successful professional career. For example, he stepped up
to be the basketball coach when Sarah was in third grade, making the sacrifice of having to leave work early for practice. His
primary motivation for doing this was so he and Sarah could
have an activity they do together. They often go out to dinner before practice so they have time to talk and catch up. He
has been doing this for three years now, and in addition to a
winning record, he has won points with Sarah for the father-
daughter time they spend together.

Michael's dedication to Hannah is endearing and he is a fierce advocate for her in all aspects of her life. It is important to him for Hannah to be included in our family activities, the Church, and in the community. When we went to the beach this past summer, he bought Hannah an inflatable boat so she could play in the ocean and dubbed it "adaptive surfing." He reached out to the head of the developmental basketball program at St. Joseph's Catholic Church and forged a relationship that made Hannah the first child with an intellectual disability to participate alongside her typical peers. Recently, we took Hannah to a Florida Gator's basketball game and the team invited all of the kids to go down to the court and shoot layups after the game. Michael left a close game during the last minute to sign Hannah up to shoot and then lifted her up to help her make a basket. (Well, almost make a basket . . . the 10-foot rim was too tall for his 6'4" frame!)

Michael and I had the opportunity to give our testimony to a prayer group at our church about how our faith journey was affected by being the parents of a child with special needs. Michael spoke about a moment when we were standing in the commons of our church watching one of our priests, who was leaving the church, give a blessing to Hannah and an adult woman with Down syndrome, Stephanie. His words were, "May you continue to show the face of Christ." Most of us aspire to be more Christ-like, but the priest told Hannah and Stephanie to "continue to show the face of Christ" to others. Michael said this was the moment that Hannah's purpose was confirmed to him and to us, and it was up to us to make sure we put her in a position to carry out this most important work of the Lord.

What makes your marriage work so well?

We have come to learn that no marriage is as perfect as the white picket fence that can be seen from the exterior of a home! The picture of marriage that is portrayed in the media and in society is unrealistic and superficial. I still remember from our Engaged Encounter the statement that "Love is a decision," and this could not be more true in the makings of a successful marriage.

Our marriage has come to work well because we both have worked diligently to make it work! We both take the commitment we made to each other before God and our family and friends very seriously. We have faced some larger-than-life obstacles as parents and as spouses and are proud that we are still standing together, better and stronger for having done so. Our marriage was tested many times, not only by the stress of health problems with Hannah but by the same issues that many other married couples face. They were just magnified by our situation. We proactively sought guidance and counsel to address our issues and made time to do this together.

Another thing that makes it all work is that we prioritize spending quality time together over doing typical household chores or running errands on the weekend (which explains the reference to the messy house above!). Hannah has taught us that tomorrow is not a guarantee and that each day is to be celebrated, so we try to spend our time enjoying each other and our children without regard to the distractions that often make it difficult to do so. We are frequent users of babysitters since we don't have a lot of family in town, and we enjoy spending kid-free time together as often as we can. We both have become less into what we want as individuals over the years and put what is best for us as a couple and a family in the forefront.

14

WHERE I SHOULD BE
David Rizzo

*The LORD is my light and my salvation; whom
shall I fear? The LORD is the stronghold of my life;
of whom shall I be afraid?*
— Psalms 27:1 —

The last thing I ever expected in my life was to be the father of a child with special needs. I wasn't prepared for it. I was caught completely unaware like a character in an old Western movie, crossing a mountain pass on horseback and greeted by rounds of rifle fire from bandits hidden in the hills.

My wife Mercedes and I were overjoyed when Danielle was born. She was our third child, our first girl. As a toddler she was full of energy. I remember how at two or three years old she would pull one of the kitchen chairs up to the counter-top and climb on it to reach items we both thought were safely out of reach. What a problem solver she seemed to be! She was fearless, especially on the swing set in our neighborhood. She would swing higher and faster than any kid her age. And though it seemed odd that she couldn't talk yet, my parents reminded me that I was a very late talker too. I was four years old before I was able to put a full sentence together.

So when people began to suggest that my beautiful daughter had autism, I thought they were nuts. I'll never forget the day I got angry at the occupational therapist from the Early Inter-vention program for bringing this up. It didn't matter that I was a physical therapist and should have known better. I was in denial. Then one day when Danielle was watching a video on television, I noticed that she insisted on watching it with the TV set to the wrong channel so that everything was distorted: all the colors, shapes, and sounds. When I set the television to the correct channel she started to cry and turned it back. When that happened I admitted to myself that Danielle did, indeed, have autism. And although it took several months of doctor's appointments and tests before she was formally diagnosed, I knew it in my gut. The reality of the situation had become just too obvious for me to maintain that nothing was wrong.

I was devastated. The year or two after Danielle was diagnosed with autism was a time of extreme isolation and sadness. Not only was Danielle completely nonverbal, but she also displayed challenging behaviors like putting non-edible items into her mouth. Sometimes it was all we could do just to keep her safe. Autism had turned my family's life upside down. It felt like my true daughter had disappeared and a changeling was left in her place. I entered a zone of numbness where I thought I could hide from my daughter's disability and the pain it brought to me and my family.

My faith in God was being seriously challenged. I wanted God to cure Danielle of her autism and make her talk. At the time, I couldn't see any meaning or purpose in her autism at all. But I knew I would have to turn toward God and my daughter in a deeper way in order to find it and to restore the joy and vitality that had disappeared from my life. I realized I could not hide away, but needed to accept the reality of my life as the father of a child with a severe disability. This meant becoming more present to my daughter, wife, and family, not less so. Also, I needed to become more present to God and His workings in my life. I had to learn to trust that God had given us Danielle for a reason, and that our lives would be enriched by having her in our family.

Looking for answers, I turned to the sacraments and sacramentals of the Church, and to prayer. As Danielle was unable to speak, I paid extra attention to finding God in the silence with her. We'd sit before the Blessed Sacrament or walk amid life-sized statues of Jesus and Mary in the rosary garden of a nearby monastery. We would kneel together in silence after receiving Holy Communion. These and other practices led to the deepening awareness of the presence of God in our lives. In a very real way, Mercedes and I started to see silence as a place to encounter God, which helped the two of us find some meaning in Danielle's silence. Her inability to speak in words began to make more sense to us, and we were able to see that Danielle was exactly who God meant her to be, and that like all of us she was made in the image and likeness of God.

The challenges of being the father of a child with autism began to change me and force me to re-examine other areas of my life, including work. At the time I was a physical therapist rehabilitating elders in nursing homes. I loved doing this but really wanted to work with people more like Danielle. So it wasn't long before I started working with adults and children with developmental disabilities. I have never regretted this decision. It has given me the opportunity to help people with a wide range of cognitive, behavioral, and physical issues. More importantly, it has taught me to see Christ in them.

One particular example stands out in my memory. I had recently started treating a young eighteen-year-old man. He weighed perhaps forty-five pounds and was born with a genetic disorder that caused extreme weakness and tight, spastic muscles. This young man was too weak to stand on his own and could not even keep his head and trunk up without some type of support. I would put him in a special body brace and standing frame. One day his mother and I strapped him in and tilted the stander to near vertical. When I looked over at him, his feet resting on blocks and his sagging trunk and outstretched arms, I was struck by how much he seemed like Jesus hanging on the Cross. This was, to me, nothing short of an encounter with Christ.

Raising a child with special needs affected my marriage too. I had to become more responsive and present when Mercedes needed me. This took some time, as we men don't always real-ize how much needs to be done or when the burden is not being evenly shared. This is especially true with child rearing, and becomes even more important when you add the demands of caring for a child with special needs. Parents need to work to-gether and help each other so neither ends up exhausted, over-whelmed, or depressed. I had to learn to schedule my work time around meetings with the child study team, school holidays, doctor appointments, and other commitments. Sometimes I had to help with our other kids since Mercedes could not be in two places at once; Brendan had Boy Scouts, Colin played sports, and Shannon acted in plays. My life was very busy. But I needed to do these things if we were to have a functional house-hold. I like to think we both learned to depend on each other more and that our marriage was strengthened by this.

The increased supervision Danielle required affected our ability to spend time together as a couple. It was hard just to go out to dinner or to a movie together because we had no one to watch Danielle. The safety issues limited the availability of babysitters, so we didn't go out much. I wish we had worked harder in those years finding opportunities to get out by our-selves, just the two of us. Nowadays, with the kids older and Danielle's behavior much improved, it's easier for us to get away and relate to one another as a couple, not just as par-ents—and it affects how we feel about each other and how we feel about ourselves. It also reminds me of when we were dating and carefree.

Danielle is sixteen now and continues to learn more and more every day. She has learned to communicate using an elec-tronic speech machine that turns the pictures she selects into sentences. At other times she uses sign language. Her behaviors have improved and she no longer puts inedible objects into her mouth. She follows basic directions and participates in family and school activities. One of her favorite activities is figure skating for the Special Olympics. And to our delight she attends Church regularly and receives the Holy Eucharist. She is a cherished and important member of our family.

I'd like fathers of children with disabilities to know that our children are wonderful in their own right, and if we remain open to them and participate in their lives, we will be changed by their presence and by their love. I'd like the fathers of younger children to be assured that where you are now is not where you'll be in ten years. There will be highs and lows, but in the end you will be glad that you are a part of your child's life and that your child is a part of yours. It is important to have faith in the journey and to be receptive to the activity of God as you walk the path in front of you.

I am still walking my path and continue to struggle as I go from point A to point B. Life is not linear. At best it's two steps forward, one step back. Sometimes it is a spiral. Other times, a leap. Sometimes it spins me around as if I'm blindfolded, like in a game of pin the tail on the donkey. I continue to make mistakes as I go, and I am far from a perfect father and husband. However, I trust that if I stay on the path that God has laid out for me, I will get to where I am supposed to go.

I have hopes and dreams for my family as I walk the path. First, I hope they know that I love them, even when I do make mistakes and lose my temper or fail to treat them like the gifts they are. I hope they know that I am truly sorry and will earnestly try to do better. My dream for Danielle is that she grows into the unique person God intends her to be and is able to live her life to the fullest. I pray that she never loses her fun-loving spirit or her sense of joy. I pray that she experiences the image and likeness of God within her. Perhaps the biggest hope I have for Brendan, Colin, and Shannon is that they don't feel locked into viewing themselves solely as siblings of a child with autism. Lastly, I hope Mercedes forgives me my failings and doesn't feel overwhelmed or alone in the struggle.

Being the father of a child with special needs isn't something I would have had the courage to choose, but fortunately, it was not up to me. It was up to God. There are so many things I don't understand in my life and this is one of them. It wasn't something I could flee from or wish away, though I tried to do both. I had to learn to trust that I could be the father that God is calling me to be. It hasn't been easy. There are nights I stand on my driveway and look up at the stars and wonder, "Why me?" I feel silly standing there waiting for the stars to answer. I stand in the silence and darkness, waiting for the heavens to open and the voice of God to thunder something definitive. Sometimes I hear the wind or an owl, and I strain to make out what God is trying to tell me. After several minutes, I turn back to the house and sit down next to Danielle as she shakes a plastic water bottle back and forth. She does this every now and then and it calms her down. I realize her autism is as mysterious as the stars and as silent as God. But it is here, in the silence, that I am accustomed to enter into communion with Danielle, my beloved daughter, and with the God who has chosen me to be her father. I do not understand it, but I know that this is where I should be, and nowhere else.

David Rizzo is the author of Faith, Family, and Children with Special Needs: How Catholic Parents and Their Kids with Special Needs Can Develop a Richer Spiritual Life *(Loyola Press, 2012). David is a physical therapist and father of four children, one of whom has autism.*

15

LEADERSHIP LESSONS FROM A CHILD WITH AUTISM

*In the Divine solicitude for children was the
affirmation that there are certain elements in
childhood which ought to be preserved in the
highest manhood; that no man is truly great unless
he can recapture something of the
simplicity and humility of the child.*
— Archbishop Fulton Sheen —

Dads, do we ever think about the positive impact our children can have on other areas of our lives? It is easy to get lost in the daily emotional, spiritual, physical, and financial battles, but when we stop and reflect on how these experiences have shaped us, we can often see tremendous blessings in our lives. I recently reflected on the impact my oldest son has had on my business career.

I have been leading people since I began working at a local restaurant when I was sixteen years old. Leadership has always been a passion for me, and after years of study, reading dozens of leadership books, listening to mentors, and accumulating great experience on the way to a successful career, I have come to understand one thing: I can still learn something new about leadership. In my case, the best source of ongoing leadership lessons is my seventeen-year-old son Alex.

With roughly 1 in 68 children diagnosed with autism (1 in 42 boys and 1 in 189 girls), it is likely you have parents in your extended circle of family and friends who are raising a child on the autistic spectrum. For clarification, and perhaps education purposes, you should be aware that people suffering from autistic spectrum disorder will always manifest the disorder differently. These wonderful people are all unique and their symptoms can range from very low-functioning and nonverbal to very bright and verbal. A disorder that includes such a broad and varied range of symptoms is often called a spectrum disorder; hence the term "autism spectrum disorder."

The most significant and commonly shared symptom is in the area of social communication, which includes challenges with direct eye contact, normal conversation, communicating ideas, empathy, and reading facial expressions or social cues.

My wife and I love Alex and his younger brother Ryan more than words can say and we've always tried to protect them as best we can. We have both discussed Alex's condition and challenges openly with friends since his diagnosis fifteen years ago, but I feel compelled to share with others how he has inspired me to be a better person, a better father, and certainly a better leader in my work life.

It dawned on me not long ago, after playing his favorite game of Trivial Pursuit and listening to an endless series of questions about my favorite foods, favorite songs, and favorite Mythbusters episodes, that the way I interact with and lead Alex has strong parallels to leadership in the business world. Did it ever occur to you that an additional blessing of having a child with special needs can be seen in our careers?

The skills I have developed and the lessons I have learned in working and communicating with Alex have been spilling over into my professional life for years. So, I would like to share seven vital leadership lessons I have learned from my gifted son.

1. **Be Patient.** Children with autism are just like any other children and they can try your patience! Peers, friends, and co-workers can try your patience as well. Does losing our cool ever really accomplish anything? Gaining an understanding of the motives or causes of the behavior that is causing your impatience will help you remain calm and achieve a faster resolution to the problem.

2. **Be a Clear Communicator.** Being unclear and ambiguous in communicating with kids like Alex is incredibly frustrating for them. It is a sure bet that our team members feel the same way. Be clear in sharing your thoughts; don't send an email that can be misinterpreted; have a clear vision of what

you want to accomplish in your communication; and always, always, always avoid ambiguity and vagueness. Having a trusted proofreader around can be helpful!

3. **Be Fair.** Kids on the autistic spectrum require a lot of attention. Driving to therapists, providing structured and predictable days, facilitating appropriate conversations with others, dealing with a limited diet . . . the list is endless. Making sure our other son gets equal time and attention is a constant source of concern in our home. This has made me very sensitive to fairness in the workplace. Don't play favorites, listen to all sides of an issue, give equal time, etc. An even-handed approach in your business and personal relationships will earn you trust and credibility over the long term.

4. **Honor Commitments.** If you say you will do something, you can bet kids with autism will remember . . . and hold you to it. We have to be very careful about announcing everything from future family events to what we are having for dinner. This has taught me to be very careful about honoring my commitments in the workplace. It is difficult, but colleagues and the people on our teams deserve this courtesy. Alex relies on my commitments, why shouldn't everybody else?

5. **Celebrate Diversity.** Alex is different and we have learned to celebrate his differences and recognize the special gifts he has to offer the world. Look around your organization. There are people with special skills, who come from different generations, who have different ethnic backgrounds and celebrate different religions. I am describing something

bigger than traditional race and gender diversity. Our organizations are filled with unique and special people who have great value to offer, just like Alex, and we must celebrate their differences and harness their potential. My hope is that one day the world will advance enough in its thinking to welcome, celebrate, and find the great value in Alex and other children with special challenges.

6. **Speak Up and Get Involved.** Having a child with special needs will fundamentally alter your outlook on life—ask anyone who is raising one of these gifts from God and I believe you will hear a similar view. Alex has helped me recognize that he can't defend or speak up for himself without my help. Therefore, for the last few years I have been outspoken about autism and educating anyone who will listen. I also speak up and have gotten involved in a number of causes and issues that affect me, my Catholic faith, my family, and our community. How about you? What catalyst exists in your life to motivate you to speak up, get involved, and make a difference?

7. **Practice Selfless Love.** I love Alex unreservedly, as a father should love his child. This type of love was called *storge* by the ancient Greeks and is the love that exists in families, often between parent and child. But another kind of love exists between us that is called *agape*, or selfless and charitable love. Alex needs my unconditional and selfless love with no strings attached. I have learned to apply this type of love in the workplace as well. As a leader, I am here to serve my team, my company, and my clients selflessly, thoughtfully, and with a servant's heart. Try putting all of your actions

through the filter of selfless love and it will positively change you, your team, and your organization for the better.

All of us could stand to learn important lessons from our children. Alex is a child with special needs, but first and foremost he is a *special child*. The heroism he exhibits each day by simply interacting with a world that is often alien and unfriendly is a source of ongoing inspiration for me and others who have gotten to know him.

I am grateful that I have gained the humility to recognize that over the years I have been Alex's father and supposedly the teacher in our relationship, when in so many ways he has been teaching me the entire time.

16
THE ILLUSION OF PERFECTION
Chad Judice

*Enter by the narrow gate; for the gate is wide and
the way is easy, that leads to destruction, and those
who enter by it are many. For the gate is narrow
and the way is hard, that leads to life, and
those who find it are few.*
— Matthew 7:13–14 —

It was a beautiful sunny afternoon in May of 2005. I was staring into the heart of Cathedral Carmel from the back window of a Catholic elementary school in my hometown of Lafayette, Louisiana. A student posed a question to me for the ages: "Coach Judice, what is your greatest fear?" Being completely transparent I replied, "Having a child with a mental or physical handicap. I am a perfectionist and I don't know if I would handle that very well."

I moved on to another teaching position at a Catholic high school the following year, never giving that response a second thought. I didn't need to. I had a healthy six-month-old son at home and my wife had not experienced any complications in our first pregnancy. I was on top of the world, and by its standards, my life was perfect.

As a cradle Catholic, I had become entrenched in my own zone of comfort. I fulfilled my Sunday Mass obligation but chose a route of self-imposed ignorance of the difficult teachings of the Church. I had my faults, but I knew I was, overall, a nice guy. I was living the American dream and in control of my future.

My perception of reality was about to change drastically. When I began teaching at St. Thomas More Catholic High School, I met men who not only wore their Catholic faith on their sleeves, but invited other men in a loving challenge to do likewise. Being in their presence created a desire to possess what they had—and whatever it was was so real it was contagious.

Joining a prayer group with these men, my brothers in Christ, became the foundation for me to come to terms with my own brokenness and to recognize a selfish mentality that had taken root in my soul.

As my time with these men increased and my faith deepened, so did my keen awareness of the need for prayer and discernment. My wife Ashley was beginning to yearn for a second child, but she was ready way before I was. Recalling all of these events now, I can say with certainty that my hesitation was driven by nothing other than selfish reasons. Many nights I struggled internally against my own self-interest and need for preservation of the status quo. Being an only child had only fostered a reliance on self in the absence of any siblings to depend on. I brought that mentality into my marriage, and after having my first child I did not feel an urgent need to have another.

Ashley and I took a second honeymoon to Mexico in May of 2008. Two weeks after returning home from our trip I received an unexpected but not unwanted present. I was going to be a father again. My "perfect" life was about to change. On September 30, 2008, within forty-five minutes in the darkness of an ultrasound room, God revealed to me His divinity and my meager humanity.

Ashley was in the middle of her second trimester. The ultrasound for our oldest son Ephraim had been one of the most memorable experiences from her first pregnancy. We could see Ephraim's heart beating, all of his internal organs, and learned his gender.

This time around, I remember Ashley asking not to be informed of the baby's gender until we knew it was healthy. When the ultrasound began I could see a confused and concerned look on Ashley's face as well as the tech's. I asked intently, "Is everything okay?" She replied, "I'm just having trouble locating a few things," and then quietly walked out of the room. Moments later a second tech entered in her place, and as she picked up where her predecessor had left off, those same looks returned. Unaware of Ashley's request, she said quietly, "It's a boy." She never said he was healthy.

Ashley's obstetrician entered the room and with a solemn look stated, "I am sorry to tell you this, but we could not locate part of your son's brain known as the cerebellum. We are not sure what is wrong, but tomorrow a Maternal Fetal Specialist will confirm what the problem is."

The following day my greatest fear became my reality. Our unborn son had been diagnosed at sixteen weeks with a birth defect known as spina bifida. This is a neural tube defect (a term for one's spinal cord) that occurs in the first six weeks of pregnancy. There are different types of spina bifida with different degrees of severity. Our unborn son had been diagnosed with the most severe form. The projected quality of life based on medical literature and the severity of this condition painted a less than encouraging picture. We learned that 80 percent of couples who receive the diagnosis at this point in the pregnancy choose abortion. Roughly 75 percent of children with a birth defect this severe cause a miscarriage before twenty weeks. As my wife read further, it became clear that should he survive the entire pregnancy, he would need major surgery on his spinal cord and brain within twenty-four to seventy-two hours after birth. According to the information, even if procedures post-birth were completely successful, he would never walk, be severely mentally disabled, and his life would be riddled with excessive health issues.

My wife sat across from me with tears running down her face. I can only imagine what thoughts were crossing her mind. She is a Neonatal Intensive Care Unit (NICU) nurse at a local hospital and cared for premature babies with multiple health issues on a daily basis. In this case her knowledge was more of a curse than a blessing. Raising her tearful eyes she said, "I am going to hell!" I replied, "Ashley, what are you talking about?" She said, "I am actually thinking about aborting this baby."

At this point, had I not been engaged in a deeper way in my Catholic faith and been one with our Lord in the Eucharist, I would not have been empowered to love like Jesus did or be willing to lay down my life for my bride as He did for His on Calvary. I grabbed Ashley and said, "This is not your fault. It's not my fault. We were sent this child for a reason. We have to trust in God, the way Ephraim trusts in us." I was referencing the places in the Gospels where Jesus calls us to have childlike trust in order to enter the kingdom of heaven. Facing these types of circumstances amidst the fear of the unknown will test one's faith beyond the realm of description. Fear could have turned to anger and bitterness for the unfair situation we were in, but instead love drove us to a point of selflessness that was not possible without divine intervention.

What is love? We use that word in so many cavalier ways it has lost its meaning. I love ice cream, but not the way I love Ashley. Real love has less to do with how one feels; real love is a decision. "He who does not love does not know God; for God is love" (1 Jn 4:8). Only when I made that decision to love and trust in God—and only because of that decision—could Jesus Christ transform my life.

The following day that decision was reinforced as the words I had referenced to Ashley were read out loud in the Gospel at our weekly school Mass: "Truly, I say to you, unless you turn and become like children, you will never enter the kingdom of heaven. Whoever humbles himself like this child, he is the greatest in the kingdom of heaven. Whoever receives one such child in my name receives me" (Mt 18:3–5).

God had my attention! After Mass a good friend and campus minister invited the entire school community to pray for a miracle. Broken and weeping, we embraced. I know it was one of the most powerful things all of the students had ever seen, especially the young men. In that embrace I realized God had brought me to nothing, so that in the midst of my nothingness I could find Him. I had given God parts of my life, the parts I was comfortable with. I understood He wanted it all. Surrender was no longer a mere option, it was a necessity.

That surrender began a journey of faith, hope, love, and the power of prayer with the St. Thomas More Catholic High School community—one that illustrated Christ did not come to take away my suffering, but would be with me in it every step of the way—not because He needed my suffering, but to give me the opportunity to become more like Him. Embracing my suffering and cross allowed Christ to replicate what He did with His own: He took what this world would define as a tragedy and turned it into a triumph. "And he said to all, 'If any man would come after me, let him deny himself and take up his cross daily and follow me.' For whoever would save his life will lose it; and whoever loses his life for my sake, he will save it" (Lk 9:23–24).

Venerable Archbishop Fulton Sheen once stated, "Unless there is a Good Friday in your life, there can be no Easter Sunday." Easter Sunday came February 17, 2009 at 9:30 a.m. My second son, Elijah Paul Judice, was born. He had defied all medical odds throughout the pregnancy and continued to do so afterward.

Eli has become the catalyst of change in the lives of so many others, especially our family. No change, however, has been more drastic than mine. I had developed crafty ways to hide my imperfections from others. My son's inability to hide his imperfections and his humility in accepting them with joy has taught this teacher and father the greatest lesson of all: Eli was never the one who was broken and needed to be healed. God used Eli to heal me. "Those who are well have no need of a physician, but those who are sick. . . . For I came not to call the righteous, but sinners" (Mt 9:12–13).

Fatherhood and all that it encompasses has been the heart of my journey to full union with the Catholic Church. My oldest son's birth in January 2005 brought into focus the concept of the love of God the Father. I had never loved anyone or anything the way I loved him. I finally understood what I had heard my whole life, "God the Father loves you." God was my heavenly Father as I was Ephraim's earthly one. My journey with Eli peeled away the hardness of my heart and allowed the fullness of Truth to replace it. It was His grace that empowered me to embrace my cross and choose to authentically die to self for the first time in my life. The reciprocated love in response to that gift then breathed the life of the Holy Spirit into my marriage and transformed it into what the Church always intended it to be.

In November of 2013, Ashley and I began a familiar but unexpected journey. News that we would be welcoming a third child into our family was joyful yet challenging. Joyful because Eli had opened my eyes to the intrinsic value and the gift of every human life. Challenging because of the anticipation of the twenty-week ultrasound and the call to higher levels of self-denial to make an increasingly complicated situation work.

After facing my greatest fear with Eli, many would have understood the logic of foregoing a third pregnancy. However, the fruits of the Spirit in my marriage produced a quiet confidence and trust in God's plan and His love in my life. "There is no fear in love, but perfect love casts out fear. For fear has to do with punishment, and he who fears in not perfected in love" (1 Jn 4:18). On July 16, 2014 I welcomed a third son into the world, a healthy baby boy named Ezra Matthew Judice. Call me old fashioned, but the 1960s television program *My Three Sons* really resonates in my current life circumstances.

Now I can see that I chased the illusion of perfection my entire life believing that it was the one thing that validated my existence. God used the imperfections of a child with spina bifida to help me realize that although as a father and husband I may never be perfect, in Christ my love is.

Chad Judice is an award winning author and national speaker. To contact him or to order his books, Waiting for Eli *and* Eli's Reach, *please visit his website:www.chadjudice.com.*

17

THE ROLE OF FATHERS

A Candid Interview with Jeanne Lyons
Teacher, Consultant, and
Advocate for Children and
Families with Special Needs

Jeanne, over the many years you have been involved in helping children with learning and
developmental challenges integrate into the
Catholic faith, how would you describe the role
of the father in these families? Do fathers need
to be more engaged?

I feel like I've seen a fairly wide range of levels of engagement
on the part of the dads of kids with special needs. There was
the couple whose divorce seemed to stem largely from the dad's
rejection of the diagnosis of their child's developmental disability and the mom's frustration with the dad not allowing the
child to receive needed therapies, watching precious time slip
away as their child went without assistance and solidified hab-
its that would only become more and more difficult to undo.
Then there are dads who single-handedly bring their children
with disabilities to my free, inclusive music classes at church,
and have clearly worked hard at learning from their child's
therapists. These dads have become very skilled in effectively
and lovingly assisting their children with their struggles and
in making the most of the gifts that always go hand-in-hand
with disabilities.

However, in the special needs parent support group that
meets at our church, the attendance is almost always exclusively female, even though free, highly skilled childcare is always
offered. Whenever a dad does attend and participates in the
invaluable networking and information sharing that occurs at
these meetings, the moms always express their great admira-
tion for these fathers who break the mold and participate in
the meeting with their wives. You may notice that I said, "the

meeting." When that lone dad attends a meeting, he isn't very likely to return, even if he seemed to get a lot out of that first meeting. I think this speaks to the need for support groups geared specifically for dads.

> What keeps men from accepting their respon-
> sibilities as fathers and husbands in these fami-
> lies? What are the challenges for them?

Some dads seem to have what I view as a tragically misguided feeling that they somehow need to defend their child/wife/ family from a diagnosis or from concerned professionals— that as the protector of the family, the dad should somehow keep "the threat" at bay or keep it from "ruining things" for their loved ones. This can be so sad when, consequently, a child ends up being denied early intervention during crucial years when therapies often have the most power to improve outcomes for that child.

Because of the genetic component of autism and how it currently seems to be much more prevalent in males, I sometimes see dads of children with high-functioning autism who perceive that their children are just doing the kinds of things they did as a child. These dads might have high-functioning autism features of their own, symptoms that were viewed, mistakenly, as character flaws when they were growing up. These symptoms or behaviors were often treated with authoritarian disciplinary methods back in the day. I've heard such dads making statements like, "My child doesn't have autism. He's just doing the same kind of things I did when I was young. My parents were able to 'straighten me out.'" This usually means that the dad has ended up with a job that pays well, but might not be aware of other issues that he has, not just from his own autistic features, but from not having ever received appropriate treatment for them. So a dad like this is likely to view a child's diagnosis (or the idea of a possible diagnosis) and the prescribed therapies as just modern-day inventions that coddle children, or as a societal tendency to pathologize everything, wasting time and money.

Speaking of money, the expense involved in meeting the needs of a child with a disability can be overwhelming and unending. A primary breadwinner dad may just shut down in the face of such daunting expenses. "Give us our daily bread" comes to include "Give us our weekly occupational therapy, physical therapy, behavioral therapy, social skills coaching, feeding therapy, etc." This can push a dad to exercise his capacity for trusting God to the most strenuous degree. When a dad rises to meet that challenge to trust, the whole family benefits as a unit and as individual members who flourish from witnessing such a beautiful example; but even the best dads experience moments when they feel crushed by the weight of it all.

I also think it is much harder for dads than it may be for moms to come to terms with disabilities that are diagnosed more from behaviors than from blood tests, medical testing, or a child's physical features. Autism is by far the most prevalent diagnosis among the families with which I work, and as of yet, there is no definitive medical test for autism. Sadly there are still many pediatricians who do not pick up on the early signs of autism and still respond to a mom's concerns by advising her to wait and see—which denies the child the possibility of receiving the most effective intervention, which is *early* intervention.

If a dad is the family's primary breadwinner and has not decided to also learn the skills necessary for being a primary parent as well, he may miss out on opportunities to experience extended periods of being alone with his child, as well as opportunities to parent that child while the child is interacting with other kids the same age. If the dad only spends short spurts of time with his child and relies on his wife to be the one bearing the parental vigilance even during these short spurts, he is not going to notice the full impact of behavioral/sensory differences in that child. His wife will bear the brunt of these differences as she spends most of her waking hours caring for that child, seeing how he or she is different from other children around the same age. While she gradually develops the gut feeling that something is wrong, the dad will not see it, and even wonder why she "can't handle things" as well as most mothers. Receiving a pediatrician's advice to wait and see gives the medical-data-seeking dad even more support for not believing in his wife's instinct about their child.

What happens in the families when the father is fully engaged? How does this impact the children, the marriage, and the overall family dynamic?

While my husband Rory didn't start out being fully engaged, once he stepped up to the plate he did so in an awesome way. A moment that stands out for me is one day when he picked up our son Shawn (who has high-functioning autism) after a Saturday morning of Outdoor Sensory Adventures, a therapeutic hiking experience developed by Clay White. I believe Shawn was around eight years old at the time. Shawn's friend Charlie, who had the same diagnosis as Shawn, had also been in the group that morning. Both boys were science guys and had some of the most intriguingly nerdy, amazingly intelligent conversations together. When Rory and I were talking after he brought Shawn home, Rory said something like this, "I would really like to take just Shawn and Charlie hiking together. I bet I could find some ways to get them to socialize better with each other and really play together. I think it would help them both."

Whenever that moment replays in my mind I almost see a heaven-sent ray of light piercing through the clouds and illuminating my husband's blondish hair. His blue eyes were the most dazzling shade I have ever seen, and there were definitely angel voices singing in the background. Rory did take the boys on that hike and many more fun activities after that (wrangling through all the autism meltdowns and behavior minefields along the way). My husband became a rock star of fatherhood.

Our younger son, Riley, only required a few years of occupational therapy, speech therapy, and social skills coaching, and his diagnosis ended up as sensory integration dysfunction, which today is called sensory processing disorder. (Riley was the one to receive the earliest intervention because of what we had learned with Shawn.) We then were able to replace Riley's sensory-based occupational therapy with carefully selected sports activities that would meet his need for lots of extra proprioceptive input. Riley's occupational therapy results were phenomenal, to the point of his becoming an outstanding athlete, excelling in many sports and ultimately being a kicker for his college football team. Rory loves being a sports dad, but somehow he did not let his many hours of accompanying Riley to sports practices and competitions keep him from staying involved in Shawn's non-athletic but very intense interests in plants, rocks and minerals, cats, combat robotics, and strategic role-playing card games.

Rory's commitment to staying very involved in both his sons' lives—autism and all—has paid off tremendously, both in our marriage and family life. My husband and I are a team. We have one of those complementary marriages, in which we don't have many common interests and each excels at very different skill sets. Though our differences can sometimes be frustrating, we actually work very well together and appreciate that where one is lacking, the other can do what needs to be done. I'm an arts, language, and creativity person; he's a math and systems person. We've learned from each other things that we otherwise might not have tried, and have made adaptations that we otherwise would have been more reluctant to make. Parenting together, especially with autism in the mix, has made us rely on each other and on God. We've worked well together and have also experienced times when we've actually traded the primary parenting role. For example, while I was more of the primary parent when our boys were young, that baton surprisingly passed to Rory as our boys entered college and they turned more toward their dad for advice and assistance with the challenges of college life.

I believe that because Rory stayed engaged when they were young (even while working so very hard for us to be able to pay for incredibly expensive therapies), he has become an awesome primary parent and college dad to our two handsome young men. Rory is now working hard for us to be able to pay college expenses. He has also been very supportive of my now having the opportunity to spread my wings by working on staff at our parish (using the skills that Shawn taught me) as the coordinator of Special Needs Religious Education, a job that constantly pulls me in many directions at once.

Our faith is one thing that we do have in common and this has sustained us in so many ways throughout our thirty years together, through the scary years when Shawn's diagnosis was new and through the years of advocating for him throughout his educational experiences. The stress of dealing with autism can take a big toll on a mother's health. Though I haven't developed any major illnesses, I've experienced challenges with depression, a myriad of reproductive health issues, endocrine problems, and annoying eye diseases. Rory and I have also experienced four miscarriages—two boys with trisomies and two children we won't know more about until we meet in heaven. Although all four miscarriages occurred in the first trimester of my pregnancies, our Catholic faith made those losses very real and very deep for both of us, as it also provided a source for healing. Rory was *with* me in those losses, just as he has been *with* me in parenting, *with* me in learning from and working with autism. I'm so grateful to God for giving Rory to me as a real partner in marriage, in parenting, and in our faith. Rory is steadfast and an incredibly giving person, demonstrating to me again and again the faithfulness of God.

> What role does faith play in helping these engaged dads stay on track with their responsibilities?

Parents of kids with disabilities are constantly being attacked by worries about both daily struggles and what the future will hold. Faith is the most powerful shield against these worries. Walking by faith and not by sight makes a joyful family life possible. 2 Corinthians 5:6–7 (NAB) says, "So we are always courageous, although we know that while we are at home in the body we are away from the Lord, for we walk by faith, not by sight."

Here on earth where we are "at home in the body," society does not offer much to help those with disabilities. Parents must wrestle with insurance to get needed therapies, maintain the vigilance required to try to get schools to provide the educational supports a child needs, only to deal with the 80 percent unemployment rate for adults with disabilities. We cherish our children, but society does not. Faith is what can keep a dad from giving up. Faith makes it possible for a dad to be a shepherd with his wife to help their family embrace a life of beatitude, knowing that children with special needs are shining examples of those who receive each promise of blessing spoken by Jesus in the Sermon on the Mount.

If you could sit down with a father who has just learned one of his children has been diagnosed with autism, Down syndrome, or a host of other challenges, what would you like to share with them at that moment?

You have been given a gift—a gift that you never would have chosen and a gift that many would mistakenly see as a curse. But you have a beautiful Catholic faith, and if you let that faith shape what you see—if you lean on it as if it were an immovable boulder—you will very gradually be able to recognize your child and his or her disability as an amazing, unfathomable gift from God. It's all about trust and trying to learn to see as God sees. The Bible is filled with stories where God uses those perceived as weak, or least able, to do the impossible, making it obvious that the work is God's, done through persons who are willing to trust Him enough to try their very best, to go all out for Him and for the loved ones God has given them.

Don't waste time trying to wish away a disability or fight a diagnosis, because the earlier the intervention, the more powerful it is, and the less time it may take to see significant results. It's a leap of faith because you'll never really know how much your early-as-possible work paid off compared to if you had waited until later. However, research has shown that it greatly increases your chances for as much success as possible for your child.

Shame doesn't do you or your child any good. Trying to work in secret (in the dark really) or pretending something doesn't exist uses up energy that is much better spent banding together with people who can help you or work with you. It's all about being part of the Body of Christ, the kingdom of God, in community—not hiding away or trying to work alone out of shame. Go to support group meetings, even if you're the only dad there. Tackle the potential discomfort of being the only dad in the group by rounding up and encouraging other dads of kids with special needs to come to the meetings with their wives.

Speaking of shame, do not be afraid of (or ashamed of) your child's label. Dare to speak it out loud and let your speaking it spread awareness and express respect. A wise mom of twins with special needs, Carol Wilkerson, once explained to me that people are already giving my child a label, but the labels they are using in their ignorance are labels like the following:

- the bad kid

- the weird kid

- the psycho kid

- the kid with the incompetent parents!

Wouldn't you rather have people be aware of your child's correct label, such as autism, bipolar disorder, ADHD, anxiety, dyspraxia, mitochondrial myopathy, intellectual disability, cerebral palsy, etc.? Help to remove any stigma that exists around disability labels by claiming them and speaking about them with truth, respect, faith, hope, and love. How else can harmful stigmas eventually be extinguished?

Love your child by loving your wife, working with her, supporting her efforts, letting her support your efforts—each of you making the most of the abilities that God has given you, whether or not they match up with stereotypical male and female roles. Learn how to do the diapers, laundry, dishes, and the basics of childcare because there are times when you and your wife are going to need to be a tag team. Each spouse should have the basic skills to take over and give the other a chance for some recovery.

Play with all your children, even if that play involving your special child looks very different from typical childhood play. Play helps everyone to tap into their sense of humor. (Thanks to my husband, our back yard not only became a soccer field and a football field, but the field ended up being bordered on one side by a test garden for carnivorous plants and many other really weird and beautiful plant species.) Learn to strategize with your wife the way coaches collaborate to build an awesome team. Knowing how to play and how to strategize your way through the basic situations of life is so important. Raising children requires a lot of strategy, and the level of strategizing needed is greatly increased by disabilities and special needs.

Meet with your pastor, man to man, to tell him what you need from your parish, whether it's special needs options in religious education, sensory equipment in the cry room so your family can attend Mass as a family, a respite program, the willingness of the parish school to welcome students with special needs, etc. When you meet with your pastor, bring along other dads of children with special needs. Even if your pastor is not ready to act, keep working at increasing his level of awareness until he is.

Pray with your wife and pray with your family. Your children need to see that you are strengthened by prayer and your Catholic faith, and that they can also learn how to tap into this strength.

Know that you, your spouse, and each child has their very own ministry, even (or perhaps *especially*) your child with special needs. Accept that this child may need to pray in atypical ways. For example, silence and stillness may hinder this child's prayer, whereas movement and livelier music may enhance it, or vice versa. Their natural inclinations regarding prayer may differ greatly from your own. Pay attention to this child's neurologically wired prayer preferences and be willing to attend the type of Mass that enhances your child's connection to God, whether that's the Mass with organ music or guitars and drums, with great solemnity or a more charismatic style. (For example, I've heard from some parents that the cultural expectations of children at a Spanish Mass are the best fit for their child, even though their family doesn't speak Spanish!) Talk with all your children about how there is no one right way to pray, and let them experience different liturgical styles of the Holy Mass, seeing what helps them to best reach out to God.

If you get dirty looks at Mass because of your child's behavior, explain to your pastor how this feels and how it affects your family. Ask your pastor for support in spreading disability awareness in your parish, perhaps through his homilies, and *keep on going to mass* with your family! Your child and your child's disability have much to teach, contribute to, and share with your parish family. You will be astonished to meet some of the kindest people you could ever imagine, all because of your child. These people will inspire you, just as you inspire them, and they will help you to keep walking by faith. You will also find many people, even in your own parish, who do horrendously insensitive things because their lives have been sorely lacking in opportunities to be with and learn from people with disabilities. Let your child(ren) work their ministry, and replace any of your false, outdated vestiges of shame with *pride* in their great ministerial work.

Your child has much to teach and preach in incredibly profound ways, with or without words. Let your child continue to work at his or her unique, God-given ministry, and prepare yourself to be amazed!

18

UNLESS WE BECOME AS LITTLE CHILDREN: LESSONS MY SON HAS TAUGHT ME

Joseph Pearce

Suffer the little children and forbid them not to come to me; for the kingdom of heaven is for such.
— Matthew 19:14 —
Douay-Rheims Bible

On St. Patrick's Day 2002, eleven months after Susannah and I were married, our son Leo was born. He has Down syndrome and would later be diagnosed as having autism. What a joy he has been over the past thirteen years! What a joy and what a blessing!

Father Ho Lung of the Missionaries of the Poor, whose biography I have been blessed to write, describes those with Down syndrome as "by definition, love": "They live on love, and they live to love. They are basic elemental human nature, in all its beauty and simplicity. We know that if anyone has a Down syndrome child, they can be sure that joy, laughter, and love have been given to them as a special gift from God. . . . There is no ambition, no battle for power, no pomp, no falsehood, no hypocrisy in people with Down syndrome."

As Leo's father, I know from the beauty of experience that our son is a special gift from God. He has brought joy, laughter, and love to our family, as well as challenges that are themselves gifts. It has been said that most of us are given life in order to learn valuable lessons, whereas a special few are given life in order to teach valuable lessons. How true this is. Leo has taught us so much. He has taught us to love more truly. He has taught us to give ourselves more fully. He has helped us to lay down our lives for those we love. Could he have given us any greater gift?

When Leo was only a few days old it was discovered that he had a hole in his heart that would require surgery after he was about two years old. Susannah and I decided to pray a Rosary novena to St. Philip Neri requesting his intercession that Leo's heart might be healed without surgery. For nine consecutive months we prayed this Rosary and we considered it significant that Leo's next appointment was scheduled for the day after the nine months of prayers were completed. We went to the appointment confident that our prayers had been answered. The cardiologist listened to Leo's heart with his stethoscope and informed us that the heart murmur indicated that the hole was still there. His diagnosis confirmed the medical student's diagnosis immediately before. Therefore, two independent assessments seemed to show that our prayers for healing had not been answered. Undeterred, Susannah requested an echocardiogram. The cardiologist looked surprised, and a little irritated that we should question his diagnosis. Nonetheless, Leo was given the sonogram and the doctor was somewhat mortified and no doubt embarrassed that he had been proven wrong. There was no hole in the heart! Ever since then, St. Philip Neri has been a special favorite.

By the grace of God, and it *is* only by the grace of God, I have never had any problem whatsoever with accepting our very special son. Susannah and I had decided against any of the prenatal tests that might have detected Leo's additional chromosome, so we had no idea that we were to be gifted with such a child. I first knew that Leo had Down syndrome the first time I saw his face, moments after he was born, and could see the distinctive features which make such children instantly recognizable. I heard myself saying 'so be it' with utter peace and contentment and without the slightest hint of anxiety or disappointment. I see this as a special miracle of grace poured into my heart at that very moment, the kiss of God's love for me, an unworthy sinner. I am certainly not holy, as anyone who knows me will testify, so the sense of joyful acceptance that I experienced represents one of the clearest signs of the reality of God's presence in my life. Even today, so many years later, I am in awe at the peace that was poured into me at that moment.

The real me, the miserable and selfish me who prefers the creature comforts to the sacrifice that love demands, was in evidence in March 2011, nine years after Leo was born. I had visited the center for seriously handicapped children in the ghetto of Kingston, Jamaica, run by the Missionaries of the Poor, which is appropriately named Bethlehem. Having a disabled child of my own, it might have been expected that I would be better able to cope with the intensity of visiting such a place, but I approached the center with considerable trepidation, doubting my ability to face the horror and squalor that I expected to see. Perhaps, I thought, or at least forlornly hoped, it would not be quite as horrible and alarming as I feared. It was, in fact, worse. Upon arrival, the stench of urine assaulted the nostrils and hammered its way into the senses. Seconds later the eyes met the twisted and tangled bodies of broken childhood. There, in rows of cribs, one after another, children of all ages, from babies to teenagers, wriggled and squirmed in various degrees of helplessness. To my unbaptized gaze, the sight looked almost infernal, a place where the triumph of suffering seemed to call for the abandonment of all hope. It was March 26, the day after the historical date of the crucifixion, the most hopeless date in the whole of history; the date on which Christ laid dead in the tomb and on which Creation itself screamed in the agonized silence of the vacuum created by His Real Absence. As I looked in stunned silence at the unwanted and abandoned dregs of humanity, bent by the brokenness of body or brain, it seemed to my own broken body and brain that God was indeed dead and buried. If He existed, He seemed to have deserted His creatures in the desert of their woes.

Forcing myself beyond the momentary paralysis with which I'd been struck, I approached a girl of around eight years old lying supine in her crib. As I took her hand, she returned my forced smile with a radiance of her own that transfigured the situation and exorcised the demons from my hardened heart. It was a moment of revelation. I was now seeing with clear and grace-filled eyes. Looking up at me was the radiant face of the child Jesus. ("In as much as ye have done it to the least of these my brothers, ye have done it to me.") I had managed the barest of frozen-hearted and forced smiles in an act of sullen and stubborn duty. She had returned my pathetic effort with a smile that beamed with the light and delight of heaven itself. I had given so little; she had given so much. I finally understood the priceless lesson that my own son teaches me every day. Most of us are sent to learn but some of us are sent to teach. This little girl and my own little boy had taught me a priceless lesson that I shall never forget.

This one small incarnational moment was nothing less than a reflection of the Incarnation itself. God had made Himself as helpless in the womb of a young girl in Nazareth as He had made Himself helpless in the broken mind of my son or in the broken body of the smiling young girl in the Jamaican ghetto. And, lest we forget, March 25 is the date of the Annunciation as well as the date of the crucifixion. The Jesus who was laid in the tomb on March 25 was conceived in the womb on the same date. My first infernal impressions could not have been further from the reality before me. I was not visiting a hell without hope, but was receiving a vision of heaven. I was seeing Paradise through the eyes of a child. And in the eyes of that child, the child in me was being born. Such was the miracle of birth that I received in this other Bethlehem and such is the miracle that I receive in the presence of Leo, my own beautiful child, every day of my life.

The disabled children in the center that I visited have been abandoned by their parents, much as the vast majority of children with serious disabilities are abandoned and aborted in the womb. Lamenting this deplorable state of affairs, Father Ho Lung points the finger of blame at the way in which our defeminized culture has denigrated the dignity of motherhood: "In a time when modern women are becoming like men—office-bound, businesslike, efficient, and even hard—the children of our world will lose out. They will lose compassion, tenderness, and the intuitive powers of loving without reserve, without reason, without condition." As true and tragic as these words are, it must be added that our culture also denigrates the dignity of fatherhood, with men abandoning their responsibilities to their children and to their children's mothers.

An increase in child abuse is an inevitable consequence of the abandonment of responsible parenthood. Father Ho Lung tells heart-wrenching stories of children beaten mercilessly by parents who feel handicapped by their sons' or daughters' disabilities. I am still haunted by the story of Frankie, a young man with Down syndrome, who was brutalized and ultimately deserted by his mother for being born with "the brain of a fool." When Frankie was a baby, his mother used to "hide the boy child in her back room and lock him up."

"Frankie used to sit down as if in a prison," his aunt, in her broad Jamaican dialect, told Father Ho Lung. "And when people wasn't around, him used to sweep the house and the backyard. But Violet used to take set on him; she hated him like sin. Poor Frankie couldn't do any harm. Him would just smile and say, 'Mama, don't hit me. . . .'"

Father Ho Lung recalls one of the regular visits that Frankie received from his brother, a tall slender Rastafarian, whose hair was "all dreadlocks, long and wrapped in torches, in celebration of his defiance against society": "They spent the day together. The rastaman really loves his brother Frankie. They had arms around each other all day long. When the day was done, he held Frankie's hand and wished him good-bye. Frankie enveloped his brother with a hug and mushy kiss. All the defiance of the rastaman melted away." Frankie was so overjoyed that his brother had come that he went around telling everybody.

If truth be told, I see myself as that Rastafarian, not literally of course, but in the sense that I am also a hard-hearted rebellious sinner, full of my own worries and prejudices; like that Rastafarian I am civilized and humanized by my own special relationship with a child gifted with Down syndrome.

Frankie and the other Down syndrome residents looked after by the Missionaries of the Poor are "by definition, love," says Fr. Ho Lung. "They are very special children: God's children. They live on love, and they live to love. They are basic elemental human nature, in all its beauty and simplicity. We know that if anyone has a Down syndrome child, they can be sure that joy, laughter, and love have been given to them as a special gift from God. We welcome these gifts with delight."

As the father of Leo, I can heartily endorse Father Ho Lung's words. Leo is indeed a special gift from God and he has been the bringer of joy, laughter, and love to our family, as well as the setter of many challenges, the latter of which, though painful on occasion, have benefited us more than all the laughter and joy. One of the special joys in my life is to see the way that Evangeline, our six-year-old daughter, plays with her brother. Although Leo is twice her age and twice her size, she is his big sister. She knows that he is special, different from other children. He is teaching her how to love and how to find joy in self-sacrifice. And he is teaching his parents the same thing.

Children with Down syndrome are, indeed, very special people. They are here to teach the rest of us about love, not merely in the feel-good sense in which the word is so often abused in our largely loveless world, but in the self-sacrificial sense, which is the heart of love's deepest meaning. If the true definition of love is to lay down one's life for the other, the child with Down syndrome or with other challenging disabilities teaches us how to love more fully and more truly. Can there be a greater gift to any family than the gift of this very special love? Once again, Father Ho Lung encapsulates the heart and hub of the problem of modern life and the way in which children with Down syndrome help us to solve the problem:

> There are so many worries in the world because our modern world requires that we have so much. We sophisticated people battle and compete to acquire so much, intellectually and financially. . . .
>
> There are so many goods that are there to be had; so we miss the flowers, the trees, the birds of the air, and each other.
>
> There is no ambition, no battle for power, no pomp, no falsehood, no hypocrisy in people with Down syndrome.

Referring to Garth, another man with Down syndrome at the center run by the Missionaries of the Poor, Father Ho Lung connects the beautiful simplicity of those with Down syndrome with the beautiful and simple things in life: "I find in him the way to regain innocence. With him, I can delight in Brother Sun, Sister Moon, the pelicans, and the clouds sailing in the clear blue sky. And I can float on the ocean of faith, buoyed up by God's grace and His fatherly love."

For Father Ho Lung, as for all people who see those with Down syndrome with the eyes of love, Frankie, Garth, and Leo are not only blessings to those fortunate enough to know them but are teachers of a priceless truth about God and His Creation. Their greatest gift is that they teach us to regain our own childlike innocence. It is in their innocence that we rediscover our own. There is no greater gift that any child can give his parents. Susannah and I are blessed indeed!

I began this little meditation on my relationship with Leo, the happiest member of our family, with a quote from the Gospel: "Suffer the little children and forbid them not to come to me; for the kingdom of heaven is for such." I'd like to end with another quote from the Gospel, which I think encapsulates the glory and blessing of being gifted with a disabled child:

> And Jesus calling unto him a little child, set him in the midst of them,
>
> And said: Amen I say to you, unless you be converted, and become as little children, you shall not enter into the kingdom of heaven.
>
> Whosoever therefore shall humble himself as this little child, he is the greater in the kingdom of heaven. (Matthew 18:2–4, Douay-Rheims Bible)

Joseph Pearce is the director of the Center for Faith and Culture at Aquinas College in Nashville, Tennessee. He is the author of many books and appears regularly on EWTN and Catholic radio.

19

A Courageous Young Man and a Loving Parish

Randy Hain

On a Sunday not long ago, I had an opportunity to witness a very special moment at my parish. A seventeen-year-old man with high-functioning autism was taking his first turn as a lector at the 7:30 a.m. Mass. The lector role is an important one with serious responsibility, but this young man showed confidence and little fear as he read a very long first reading from Exodus to the several hundred people in attendance. The compliments he received after Mass for the great job he did from countless well-wishers brought a shy smile to his face as he basked in the glow of the kind words shared by his fellow parishioners.

This is a heart-warming story to be sure, but there is more here than meets the eye. There was a small army of loving and caring people in the parish who trained, supported, encouraged, and prayed for him to get to this wonderful moment of personal success on Sunday morning. The names might not mean anything to you, but people like Jeanne, Monsignor Peter, Deacon Scott, Father Tom, Deacon Mike, Sue, Rosemary, and others who helped him are the ones who have modeled the very best of what it means to be Catholic. They represent in their actions and words the elements of a caring family so critical for a thriving Catholic parish.

The young man's mother, father, and brother looked both anxious and proud as they watched him achieve this brief moment of triumph. What did this mean to them? Did they envision this day was possible in the early years after his diagnosis with autism when a normal future for their son looked bleak? How few are the little victories like this in families with special needs children? They must long for an opportunity to see their oldest child excel in life and receive accolades for achievements that other families may sometimes take for granted.

I was deeply touched by the courage of the young man for even attempting such a thing. Knowing something about autism, I realize the incredible effort he had to make to do something many of us would have seen as easy or routine. Nothing is easy for these children or adults on the autism spectrum, and they often struggle to fit in to a world they find alien and sometimes hostile. His example has inspired me, and has already helped me be more sensitive to other people I encounter each day with the great burdens they may have on their shoulders. I pray I never take for granted the things I can do, which others cannot.

This special young man is named Alex, and I know him well because he is my son. My wife and I are blessed beyond measure to be his parents and are very proud of our oldest child. Maybe, just maybe, the breakthrough he had that Sunday will be one of many in the years to come. We pray that a future we once saw as limited by autism will be blessed by God to bear much fruit for Alex, for those who love him, and for the people he encounters in his life.

CONCLUSION

There is a Great Father Inside of You

My firstborn son Alex was twenty-seven months old in late 1999 when we received the diagnosis that he had autism. My wife Sandra and I struggled to make sense of this news and understand how this could have happened, even though we suspected something was wrong because of numerous developmental delays. I think we can all agree that there is no guidebook for what to do in the event our child is diagnosed with a disability.

As a husband and father, this was not the diagnosis I expected or wanted. I was not sure what to do and I felt a mix of anger, guilt, numbness, and fear. I was the guy who always had a plan, but now I was lost. I am incredibly grateful for my wife's selfless dedication to Alex's care back in those difficult early days. Alex could not have a more passionate advocate than his mother.

This was also during my time in the spiritual wilderness before I became Catholic when I had no faith in my life. I desperately needed to pray for guidance in those challenging days, but I didn't know how.

As we began the process of getting Alex the doctors and therapists he would need, I became aware of a significant change that I did not share with anyone at the time. The wall around my heart, which had existed since my youth, had been pierced by the news of Alex's diagnosis. I was comfortable helping others but uncomfortable letting others get close to me or help me in return. I had always kept people at a distance, but this began to change after the diagnosis. At the moment my ears heard the news, I felt a deep emotional connection to my son that was unlike anything I had ever experienced. I have always loved Alex, but I believe the Holy Spirit worked through my son to begin the change of heart that eventually led me to a profound conversion and surrender to Christ in the fall of 2005 and to joining the Catholic Church with my family in 2006.

The spiritual wilderness was behind me and a new life focused on Christ and His Church was before me. My conversion began a life focused on saying yes to Christ after decades of saying no, and this new path has been life changing.

As my wife and I went about raising Alex and later his younger brother Ryan, I looked for role models and examples to follow. In Alex's early years, my father Steve was a great example of a hard-working man with strong faith and values who did whatever was necessary to provide for his family. I am blessed to have such a father who has taught me so much. As I began my journey as a Catholic, I was increasingly drawn to St. Joseph, the patron saint of fathers. Many of the lessons we can draw from this great saint are outlined in chapter one.

My brothers, I wish to leave you with some hard-earned insights from my own experiences as a the father of a child with special needs, and those I have learned from the life of St. Joseph and other great dads like the contributing writers in this book. I sincerely hope you will take these to prayer and reflect on how to incorporate them into your own lives.

A Guide for Fathers of Children with Special Needs

- Remember we are made for heaven, not this world. Let's act accordingly.

- Our vocation as husbands and fathers is to get our families to heaven.

- Keep Christ at the center of our lives, stay devoted to our Catholic faith, and pray throughout the day. We can't hope to make this journey without Christ at our side.

- The diagnosis you and your wife received was not the end of your hopes and dreams for your child, but the beginning of a wonderful and blessed life if you are open to seeking it.

- Be grateful. You were chosen by God to be the father of a child with special needs. He will not give you more than you can handle and His gift will change you for the better.

- We are not alone. Christ is always with us and is ready to help us with our burdens. The Blessed Mother and the saints, especially St. Joseph, are always prepared to intercede for us. Our wives, extended family, parish community, and other brothers in Christ will also help if we are humble enough to ask.

- Our wives need us and we need them. Don't let all of the burden fall on her. Let's be willing to go all the way, every day, in helping our families thrive and our marriages grow stronger. Divorce is not an option for us. Let's do the courageous thing and actually commit to making our marriages work!

- Pray that you will see your children with special challenges as a unique blessing given to you by God, and don't superimpose your own dreams and hopes on them. Getting this concept right will save you from frustration, anger, and guilt in the years to come.

- Accept your child and stop wishing for a better version of God's precious gift.

- Don't hide . . . behind your career, busy schedule, or the activities of your other children. We can't lose ourselves in busyness to avoid the responsibilities on our shoulders to be fully engaged in the life of our children with special needs and challenges.

- We are called to be leaders in our families and not sit on the sidelines. How are we doing in this area?

- Spend quality time with everyone in your immediate family, especially your child or children with special challenges. Play the games they enjoy, expose them to the activities they love, or simply be with them. We can't be good fathers if we keep our loved ones at a distance.

- When in doubt, engage. Don't know what to do to help your child? Engage and figure it out. Not sure what your wife needs from you? Engage and talk about it until you learn. Men, we have to *engage*.

- Be brave and do not fear. Christ is always at our side.

- Always remember that our children are God's gift to us. The love and care we show our children is our gift back to Him.

Feeling convicted? Me too. As you reflect on this book and any changes you wish to make, please be encouraged that there is a great father inside of you! Even though our lives may be more difficult than others, it takes a special man to be the father of one of these blessed children and we have been especially chosen for the role.

Our families are counting on us and we cannot let them down.

> St. Joseph, patron saint of fathers and role model for all men, please pray for us that we may always live up to your example. Please es-

pecially pray, great saint, for fathers in families with special needs children who are struggling and looking for encouragement to be the extraordinary fathers their families need them to be. Amen.

APPENDIX 1

Practical Encouragement and Wisdom

As a Catholic father dealing with all of the issues addressed in this book, I sometimes desire simple encouragement. I want somebody who has been through the same things to guide me and share their wisdom with me. The following are quotes from authors in this book, Sacred Scripture, saints, and a host of others on the topics fathers with special needs children are facing today. I hope you find this to be helpful.

Acceptance

"Practicing 'acceptance' may require a radical recalibration of our mindsets as well as complete trust and faith in God's plan for our lives. We must be faithful, humble, patient, obedient, and prayerful if we are to learn the lessons and blessings God has in store for us in our daily trials."

— Randy Hain —

"I first knew that Leo had Down syndrome the first time I saw his face, moments after he was born, and could see the distinctive features which make such children instantly recognizable. I heard myself saying 'so be it' with utter peace and contentment and without the slightest hint of anxiety or disappointment. I see this as a special miracle of grace poured into my heart at that very moment, the kiss of God's love for me, an unworthy sinner."

— Joseph Pearce —

Anxiety

"Fear not, for I am with you, be not dismayed, for I am your God; I will strengthen you, I will help you, I will uphold you with my victorious right hand."

— Isaiah 41:10 —

"Have no anxiety about anything, but in everything by prayer and supplication with thanksgiving let your requests be made known to God. And the peace of God, which passes all understanding, will keep your hearts and your minds in Christ Jesus."

— Philippians 4:6–7 —

Being Present

"I realized I could not hide away, but needed to accept the reality of my life as the father of a child with a severe disability. This meant becoming more present to my daughter, wife, and family, not less so. Also, I needed to become more present to God and His workings in my life. I had to learn to trust that God had given us Danielle for a reason, and that our lives would be enriched by having her in our family."

— David Rizzo —

Blessings

"As for me, I've changed, too. I can't say that it was just my children's autism that changed me, though. It was just my kids through and through. All of my children have challenged me, surprised me, let me down, and lifted me up. That's why kids are such a blessing from God."

— Greg Willits —

Catholic Faith

"Many families do not stay intact once a child with a disability comes into the family. Even later, stresses can fracture both the marriage and the family, and divorce occurs. If Dale had neglected his faith, that could have been us. If anything, he has grown in his faith since the birth of Mary Claire. It has drawn him closer to God."

—Patti Grieg —
(about her husband Dale)

"The Catholic faith calls us to respect the dignity of all life, in fact to be life-giving in all our actions. Once these men can see their child through the eyes of love, everything changes. This has been the message of our Lord, that our God looks on us with love, and once we accept His call to love others, we change. This is especially important for fathers of children with special needs. It is empowering and supportive for them in their role as Dad and in their role as husband."
— Monsignor Peter Rau —

"My husband's faith shows most profoundly through his actions—by the way he serves us, loves us, and puts us first in all that he does. He believes our marriage is a sacrament, our children are a gift, and our life has incredible purpose—and because of that, he inspires us all daily to follow God's will for our family."
— Lauren Warner —
wife of contributor Matthew Warner

Courage and Strength

"By nature man fears danger, discomfort, suffering. . . . Therefore it is necessary to seek brave men not only on the battlefield, but also in hospital wards, or by the sick bed of those in pain."
— Pope St. John Paul II —
General Audience on Fortitude, November 15, 1978

"It's okay to feel sad, to feel weak at times. All parents feel that way sometimes, no matter what abilities their children have. Men especially may have a hard time with those vulnerable emotions. But I encourage you to look for strength in the great-

est source, in God. With God's grace, you can be the rock and comfort for your family. You can be a great light in this world."
— Lauren Warner —

Crosses

"The Cross will not crush you; if its weight makes you stagger, its power will also sustain you."
— St. Padre Pio of Pietrelcina —

"God gives each of us our own unique crosses, each weighing exactly as much as God gives us the capacity to handle. And these crosses are not punishments, but opportunities to grow stronger, to develop richer characters, and through that, especially in raising our children, to continually grow in greater love and deeper hope in the God who loves us just as He made us."
— Greg Willits —

Family

"To maintain a joyful family requires much from both the parents and the children. Each member of the family has to become, in a special way, the servant of the others."
— Pope St. John Paul II —

"My children without disabilities know that John gets extra support because he needs it. They also know that everyone is going to get what they need. They know that John belongs to all of us and as such, we are all gifts to one another."
— Joan McCarty —

"Fathers and mothers are called to different vocations. But the experience of family life confirms how much both are needed. My children need their father. They long for their father's love. And they need their mother. They long for her too. Children— any children—remind us of the imprint of family life God has written on our hearts."

— J.D. Flynn —

Gifts from God

"We strongly believe that our increased service to others has been paralleled by Warner's significant improvement over the years. The more we advocated for insurance reform, the more Warner seemed to learn at school. The more we brought parents of children with special needs together and tried to provide them with resources and connections to those with similar challenges, the more Warner was able to engage his peers. The seemingly congruent relationship between our service to others and our child's steady improvement has helped us recognize that Warner is indeed a unique gift from God."

— Bill Jones —

"Leo is indeed a special gift from God and he has been the bringer of joy, laughter, and love to our family, as well as the setter of many challenges, the latter of which, though painful on occasion, have benefited us more than all the laughter and joy."

— Joseph Pearce —

Good Fathers

"Part of being a good father is remaining sane and faithful in the midst of this confusion. He is the wall against which the inhumanity of the world breaks, the arms which protect the young and weak. Nothing is more honorable or more manly than a father's love—day in and day out—for a child who is "imperfect" in the eyes of the world, but infinitely beautiful and precious in the eyes of God."
— Archbishop Charles J. Chaput, O.F.M. Cap. —

"I used to think that being a good father meant making sure I was doing enough for my children and my marriage, leaving the rest of my time for my own pursuits. Then I realized what an uninspiring and boring way that is to live life. Now, instead, I'm energized by the constant exploration of ways that I can give still more to each member of my family. That makes each day a new, exciting, and fulfilling challenge."
— Matthew Warner —

"It takes a special man to be a great father to any child. These gifts, given by God, are such a blessing to one's spouse and to the children. It takes a really special father to see beyond a disability. He makes no judgment about his children's successes and flaws. It is a beautiful sight indeed."
— Monsignor John F. Enzler —

Gratitude

"This habit of gratitude to God, no matter what, is really a major part of spiritual growth. It also helps fathers of special needs children to grow in holiness ourselves so we can become the fathers our children need. This is among the many ways special needs children can positively affect those around them."

— Kevin Lowry —

Heroism (and St. Joseph)

"I am convinced that focusing on the simple yet profound lessons of St. Joseph's life have helped me be a little more heroic in being a better father to both of my sons, but in particular to my son with special needs. Even when we have difficult days, I find peace and comfort in St. Joseph's intercession."

— Randy Hain —

"A father who emulates St. Joseph spends *quality* time with his family, not just time. This man is a role model to his family in living out his Catholic faith and being the light of Christ to others. This father has joy in his heart and is a man of prayer. This Catholic dad honors and loves his wife and lifts up the Sacrament of Marriage in the eyes of his children as something special and sacred. He is willing to go all the way for her and not just meet her halfway. He is fully engaged and the leader of his family."

— Randy Hain —

Illusion of Perfection

"No change, however, has been more drastic than mine. I had developed crafty ways to hide my imperfections from others. My son's inability to hide his imperfections and his humility in accepting them with joy has taught this teacher and father the

greatest lesson of all: Eli was never the one who was broken and needed to be healed. God used Eli to heal me."
— Chad Judice —

Joy in Tribulation

"When he smiled at me he looked like an angel sent from heaven . . . an angel sent to remind me that our Lord is coming and I must be ready with a joy-filled heart like that of my son."
— Randy Hain —

Joy and Fatherhood

"Imagine for a moment the son that Joseph taught carpentry is the same person who placed the stars and planets in space. The joy that Joseph knew and shared with Mary must have been indescribable. This same joy and blessing is waiting for all fathers who lead and provide for their families in accord with God's will."
— Deacon Mike Bickerstaff —

Lessons from Our Children

"I am grateful that I have gained the humility to recognize that over the years I have been Alex's father and supposedly the teacher in our relationship, when in so many ways he has been teaching me the entire time."
— Randy Hain —

"If I measure Kate's life by the most important metrics, ironically she's actually way ahead of the curve. And the truth is,

she's already taught me more about these things than I'll ever teach her."
— Matthew Warner —

Life

"Kate's birth unveiled a different path for us that we never knew existed—and now we rejoice in the opportunity and adventure of the road less traveled."
— Matthew Warner —

Love

"It is clear to me that nothing is more important to my children than the experience of our family's love. 'For a human being,' said Jean Vanier, 'love is as vital as food.'"
— J.D. Flynn —

"Real love has less to do with how one feels; real love is a decision. "He who does not love does not know God; for God is love" (1 Jn 4:8). Only when I made that decision to love and trust in God—and only because of that decision—could Jesus Christ transform my life."
— Chad Judice —

"God's love is the measure of a good life. My children's limitations remind me—daily—that whatever success the world values pales in comparison to learning to love as God loves."
— J.D. Flynn —

"When I see families who share their love with a child with intellectual differences, I am aware of both the struggle and the beauty of raising a child with special needs."
— Monsignor John J. Enzler —

Marriage

"Marriage is an act of will that signifies and involves a mutual gift, which unites the spouses and binds them to their eventual souls, with whom they make up a sole family—a domestic church."
— Pope St. John Paul II —

"Our marriage has come to work well because we both have worked diligently to make it work! We both take the commitment we made to each other before God and our family and friends very seriously. We have faced some larger-than-life obstacles as parents and as spouses and are proud that we are still standing together, better and stronger for having done so."
— Beth Foy —

Marriage and Priorities

"I'm speaking to fathers, specifically. Think about your relationship with your wife first. Although there's a temptation to put the significant needs of your child first, that's a mistake. Why? Because your marriage comes first. You share a sacrament with your wife. The children are the fruit of your blessed union. That doesn't mean that they're not important; rather, it means that your wife is super-important."
— Kevin Lowry —

"It was my faith and my godly wife that gave me the strength to live up to my responsibilities as a Catholic husband and father of a special needs child."

— Doug Keck —

Parenting

"Being a parent is not easy. But being a parent of a child with special needs is a more difficult path (sometimes lonely), one which we would sometimes like to exit. However, your family will receive many graces and blessings for which they have no comprehension. Mary Claire is a kind, sensitive, engaging, funny, and loving daughter, made perfect in His eyes. Down syndrome is only part of who she is."

— Patti Grieg —

Patience

"If you seek patience, you will find no better example than the cross. Great patience occurs in two ways: either when one patiently suffers much, or when one suffers things which one is able to avoid and yet does not avoid. Christ endured much on the cross, and did so patiently, because when he suffered he did not threaten; he was led like a sheep to the slaughter and he did not open his mouth."

— St. Thomas Aquinas —

Prayer

"How do we cope? My wife and I pray a lot. We pray for acceptance. We pray for patience and peace. We pray for the Lord

to help us be stronger parents and to help us with burdens that seem too great at times. We pray for Alex's future welfare and the future welfare of our other teenage son."
— Randy Hain —

Saints (Intercession)

"Leo was given the sonogram and the doctor was somewhat mortified and no doubt embarrassed that he had been proven wrong. There was no hole in the heart! Ever since then, St. Philip Neri has been a special favorite."
— Joseph Pearce —

Self-Sacrifice

"Real father-love is entirely a free-will act of self-sacrifice. Lived well, it gives us a window on God's own fatherhood."
— Archbishop Charles J. Chaput, O.F.M. Cap. —

St. Joseph is Our Model

"As Catholic men, we have a responsibility to be strong fathers and husbands, leaders in our parishes, good stewards in the community, and humble followers of Christ. Let's look to the inspiring example of St. Joseph, patron saint of fathers, workers, and the Universal Church for his obedience, humility, selflessness, courage, and the love he showed to Mary and Jesus. If we can emulate St. Joseph even a little each day, we will be that much closer to becoming the men we are called to be."
— Randy Hain —

Stress

"From my perspective, the stresses are financial, emotional, and physical. They worry about their child's future. They are often exhausted both emotionally and physically from their attempts to cope with regular daily life while caring for their child. Obviously, if both Mom and Dad aren't in sync and working as a team, then tension and stress comes into their relationship."

— Monsignor Peter Rau —

Suffering

"It is often difficult to see the blessings and good in any kind of suffering, yet we know from Church teaching there is redemptive power in suffering if we learn to give it up to God."

— Randy Hain —

Trusting in God

"For guys, asking for help from anyone, let alone the Lord, can be very difficult. We are supposed to be the strong ones, the ones who fix all the problems. However, in the case of a special needs child there is no *fix*, no solving the problem. There is just living and loving, laughing and crying. It is in the tough, tear-filled times when I cannot see a clear way ahead that I turn to Christ as my guide to keep me on the straight and narrow."

— Doug Keck —

APPENDIX 2

Helpful Resources

Books

- *Journey to Heaven: A Road Map for Catholic Men* (Emmaus Road Publishing, 2014) by Randy Hain

- *Faith, Family, and Children with Special Needs: How Catholic Parents and Their Kids with Special Needs Can Develop a Richer Spiritual Life* (Loyola Press, 2012) by David Rizzo

- *Be a Man!* (Ignatius Press, 2009) by Fr. Larry Richards

- *Waiting for Eli: A Father's Journey from Fear to Faith* (Acadian House, 2011) by Chad Judice

- *Candles in the Dark: The Authorized Biography of Fr. Ho Lung and the Missionaries of the Poor* (Saint Benedict Press, 2013) by Joseph Pearce

- *The Catholics Next Door: Adventures in Imperfect Living* (Franciscan Media, 2012) by Greg and Jennifer Willits

Organizations and Websites

- National Catholic Partnership on Disability
  www.ncpd.org

- United States Conference of Catholic Bishops
  www.usccb.org

- Full Inclusion for Catholic Schools
  http://www.fullinclusionforcatholicschools.org/

Helpful Articles

- "Marriage and a Special Needs Child" by Dr. Gregory Popcak — http://www.foryourmarriage.org/marriage-and-a-special-needs-child/

- "Guidelines for Sacraments for Persons with Disabilities" (USCCB) — http://www.usccb.org/beliefs-and-teachings/how-we-teach/catechesis/upload/guidelines-for-sacra-ments-disabilities.pdf

- "Life Matters and Persons with Disabilities" — http://www.usccb.org/about/pro-life-activities/respect-life-program/2011/upload/life-matters-persons-with-disabilities-bulletin-insert.pdf

Precious Treasure
The Story of PATRICK

Elizabeth Matthews never expected her son Patrick to be diagnosed with autism. But she didn't expect him to become her "escalator to heaven," either, as he was decorating the walls of the family home with mud and crayon. In *Precious Treasure: The Story of Patrick*, Matthews describes, with candor and humor, the joys, challenges, and heartaches of raising a child with special needs.

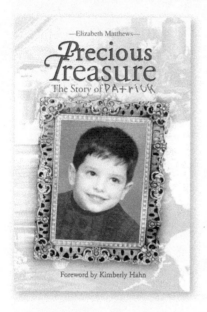

"Beth Matthews shares both her strengths and her weaknesses in such a way that you will be drawn into a glimpse of yourself. . . . And in the midst of it all, you will appreciate more deeply than before your own family and the ways in which the Lord is using your loved ones to draw your heart closer to Him."

—KIMBERLY HAHN
Author, *Life-Giving Love*

978-1-931018-13-5 // paperback